THE HISTORIC SEACOAST OF TEXAS

"THE WELCOMING COMMITTEE"
PORT ARANSAS

The HISTORIC SEACOAST of Texas

PAINTINGS BY J. U. SALVANT   ESSAYS BY DAVID G. McCOMB

UNIVERSITY OF TEXAS PRESS, AUSTIN

LIBRARY OF CONGRESS CATALOGING-IN-PUBLICATION DATA

Salvant, J. U. (Joan Usner), 1932–

The historic seacoast of Texas / paintings by J. U. Salvant ;
essays by David G. McComb. — 1st ed.

p.   cm.

Includes bibliographical references and index.

ISBN 0-292-77741-8 (cloth : alk. paper)

1. Gulf Coast (Tex.)—History—Pictorial works.   2. Gulf Coast (Tex.)—
History.   I. McComb, David G.   II. Title.

F392.G9S25   1999

976.4—dc21   98-42171

BOOK AND JACKET DESIGN AND COMPOSITION BY   Teresa W. Wingfield

PRINTING AND BINDING BY   C&C Offset Printing Co., Ltd.

(FRONTISPIECE)

THE WELCOMING COMMITTEE

No matter where you go on the coast, these "happy" creatures called laughing gulls are there to greet you. They take their job especially seriously around the ferry landings at Galveston and Port Aransas, where they greet visitors to the coast. In the summertime these creatures sport a black hood, but come winter their heads are turned to white and pale gray, as seen in the painting. They are permanent residents of the coast, feeding on sea life of all kinds; occasionally, however, they venture inland, sometimes as far as San Antonio and Austin, feeding and gathering nesting material. These gulls are one of many species on the coast; other species include ring-billed gulls and the largest species, the herring gulls. A happy memory of the coast for some is standing on the water's edge tossing bits of bread into the air as the laughing gulls scream, "Ha-ha-haah," playing their game of who gets the tasty morsel first.

CONTENTS

DEDICATION

To

JOE McCOMB,

bold traveler and intrepid explorer

ARTIST'S DEDICATION

This book is dedicated to

ROXANNE SALVANT YOUNGBLOOD,

whose great loves are warm, sandy beaches

and hot, tasty seafood!

ACKNOWLEDGMENTS

*Without the help of many people this book could never have been a
possibility. So I wish to acknowledge them and say thank you for
all the ways they have contributed to the creation of this project.*

From the Port Arthur area:
Jimmet Giron Lawrence
    Gates Memorial Library
Jill Stockinger
    Chief Librarian, Port Arthur Public Library

From the Galveston area:
Randy Pace
    Director, Residential Program
Beth Ann Weidler
    Curator of House Museums
Kurt D. Voss
    Director, Texas Seaport Museum
Kathleen Hink
    Director, Galveston County Historical Museum
Casey Greene
    Director, Special Collections—Rosenberg Library
Rabbi James Kessler
    B'Nai Israel Temple
T. J. Zalar
    Curator, Lone Star Flight Museum
Kathleen Brooks
    Librarian, Hitchcock Public Library
Dorothy and David Peterson
    Historians, Hitchcock Blimp Base
Arthur Dilly
    Executive Secretary, University of Texas Board of Regents
Petty Officers David Delgado, Shannon Fountain, and
    Charles Mallow
    U.S. Coast Guard, Galveston District
Cindy Sherrell and Jack Leo

From the Brazoria-Brazosport area:
Orren Gaspard
    Administrator, The Center for the Arts and Sciences,
    Brazosport Fine Arts Council
Gary Hall
    Park Ranger, Brazoria County Park at Quintana

From the Indianola-Matagorda Bay area:
George Fred Rhodes
    Chairman, Calhoun County Historical Society
Kathleen Rhodes Coates

From the Fulton-Rockport area:
Ellen Murry
    Texas Maritime Museum, Rockport
Kandy Taylor-Hille
    Curator, Fulton Mansion
Brent Grezintanner
    Manager; Kenneth Schwindt—Assistant Manager;
    Aransas National Wildlife Refuge
Beverly Fletcher
    Aransas National Wildlife Refuge

From the Aransas Pass area:
Rick Pratt
    Curator, Aransas Pass Lighthouse
Sidney Herndon
    Owner, Gulf King Shrimp Fleet

From the Corpus Christi area:
Don Zuris
    Director, Museum of Natural History
Jamene Toelkes and Lisa Neely
    King Ranch Museum

From the Port Isabel-Brownsville area:
Deyaune Boudreaux
    Environmental Director, Texas Shrimp Association
Chickie Henggler
    Descendant of the Champion family
Yolanda Gonzalez
    Arnulfo L. Oliveira Memorial Library at the University
    of Texas at Brownsville
Mr. and Mrs. Frank Ytturia

Others of help in creating this book are Charles and Joyce LeMaistre, L. Richard and Gale Kannwischer, Edna Phillips, Bob and Evelyn Clarke, Dale Shively and Paul Hammerschmidt of the Texas Parks and Wildlife—Coastal Fisheries Branch, personnel from the Barker History Center at the University of Texas at Austin, and the staff at the Austin Public Library.

Three people deserve much of the credit in the publishing of this work. First, my thanks goes to Gale Kannwischer, who accompanied me on several trips to the coast, provided lodging, recorded my conversations with those we interviewed, and was a very supportive companion. Second, I would like to thank David McComb for consenting to share this book with me. His wisdom and humor in writing, and his ability to paint exquisite word pictures assures the success of this book. And last, I wish to thank the most important person in my life, Dr. Edwin T. Salvant, Jr., who was my companion on many journeys to the coast, who did all of my typing and editing, and who continues to support me with patience, understanding, encouragement, constructive criticism, and, most of all, love.

ARTIST'S NOTES

The Gulf Coast has played a very significant part in my life since my earliest memories of childhood. Although we lived in New Orleans, my family owned a summer home in Ocean Springs, Mississippi, right on the beach where I spent each summer swimming, creating sand castles, and collecting conch shells. As I grew older, I began to be aware of the abundant life existing in and around the water. My father was an avid fisherman and boatman and as the sun rose on those summer mornings it would find us making our way to his special fishing spot, having already used the cast net to catch shrimp for bait. I've stood very still in ankle-deep water to watch a crab back out of its shell, then gently scooped it up for a delicious soft-shell crab dinner that night. I've been privileged to watch a stingray give birth to young, and a flounder hide itself in the sand. My father's friend owned a shrimp boat and we spent many hours helping with the day's catch, amazed to see sea horses, electric eels, and fish of every variety. And all this has made me feel one with the sea ever since I was a child.

Years later, when I moved to Texas, I lived for a time in Galveston County and once again enjoyed the closeness of the sea. By this time I had an interest in history and began to realize that history throughout the Gulf area is closely connected. La Salle came down the Mississippi River to New Orleans before he came to Matagorda Bay. Jean Laffite was a hero of the Battle of New Orleans before he was banished from Louisiana and made his way to Galveston. And then there were the Spanish explorers, the Civil War, the trade between New Orleans and the ports of Texas, the oil industry, the World War II blimp bases in both states. It was enough to excite any history buff.

After the publication of my first two books, *The Historic Forts of Texas* and *The Historic Ranches of Texas*, I felt the urge to go back to that which was most familiar to me, the Gulf Coast, and hopefully create in the paintings that which makes this part of Texas so extraordinary. It is a place that ever changes because of its unique geographic location, but also because of the impact of the people who inhabited it. My research introduced me to many of these people of the past who had a profound influence on the quality of life found on the coast—people like Rabbi Cohen, who fought the KKK, rescued prostitutes, provided food and supplies for immigrants as they arrived, visited the sick no matter what their religious conviction, and probably more than any other person set the tone for ecumenicity in Galveston which still exists today. I met, through my research, the nineteenth-century architect Nicholas Clayton, whose exquisite homes, churches, and other buildings still grace the streets of Galveston. There were the lighthouse keepers who were responsible for saving the lives of so many people, and the brothers Campioni, who served the people of the Rio Grande Valley so well. The explorers, the Indians, the pirates, the shipwreck victims, and so many others have created a rich historical heritage for the Texas Gulf Coast.

Today, the Gulf Coast exists partly because of those who have gone on before us, but also because of the many historical and preservation societies, museums, library archives, and trusts which strive to remind us of our great heritage.

Another group of extremely important people are those whose lives have been dedicated to the preservation of our natural resources. The many national wildlife refuges that dot the coast, Padre Island National Seashore, the Texas Parks and Wildlife system, and the research laboratories of the various state universities are only some of the many institutions concerned with conservation of the coastline.

The time spent in the creation of this book has been filled with experiences I shall never forget. Of special note was the day I boarded a Coast Guard cutter and was taken to the five-mile jetty lighthouse off Galveston Island. I can still feel the spray in my face and taste the salt air as we bounded over the waves, passing shrimp boats, pleasure boats, and oceangoing vessels. And as we approached the abandoned lighthouse, I couldn't help wondering how many ships it had witnessed passing by on their way to sea. Another lighthouse experience occurred the day we boarded a small motorboat to visit the Aransas Pass light. It was the coldest day that winter, barely 32 degrees, and coupled with the wind and spray from the boat skimming across the rough waters, my husband and I agreed this was the coldest we had ever been in our lives. Thank goodness for Rick Pratt, the keeper of the lighthouse. He had hot coffee and a warm fire going when we arrived. In Indianola I stood where 125 years ago a city of 20,000 people thrived, but where today only a historical marker stands, a lonely sentinel among the sea oats and sand crabs.

The creation of this book has been a time of great joy mixed with one minor frustration. It is frustrating knowing that 27 paintings are not nearly enough to show the spectacular grandeur of the Gulf Coast. Many more paintings would be required to show the entire beauty, history, and uniqueness of this complex coast. Joy was in the excitement of visiting new and familiar places, of discovering things I never knew about places I thought I knew so well. Enlightenment is always a joyful experience. This book, as well as the two previous books, has satisfied some aspect of my three loves: history, architecture, and painting.

INTRODUCTION

*I*n the black solitude at the end of the asphalt I waited in a rented white Ford sedan at Boca Chica beach, a sandy spit at the extreme southern tip of the Texas coastline. My headlights had illuminated the successive warning signs of Highway 4: "Pavement Ends"; "Road Ends, 1500 Feet"; "Road Ends, 500 Feet"; and, finally, "Stop." Beyond the last sign stretched one hundred feet of darkness that disappeared into indistinct rumbling surf. Translated from Spanish, "Boca Chica" means "little mouth," or "mouth of a girl." It marked the opening of the Rio Grande. Curiously, some 900 miles eastward in the Florida keys there is another Boca Chica. The two places, at either end of the United States Gulf Coast, are a reminder that this was once a Spanish sea.

Cautious about the loose sand, I parked facing the sea on the few remaining feet of pavement and waited to witness the sun appear over the Gulf of Mexico. The *WPA Guide to Texas,* published in 1940 and written by out-of-work historians for the New Deal, commented about this place: "Here in early days the well-to-do Spanish ranchers of Matamoros came for recreation, making the spot one of the oldest beach resorts in the United States."[1] I had tried to confirm that information in other books and with various contemporary borderlands historians, but without success. If true, it meant that Boca Chica could claim a unique place in the nation's past. But I was here for another purpose—to experience the beginning of a new day at this remote stretch of beach at the end of the Texas coast. I was curious.

At 5:30 A.M. in March 1991 there was still a three-quarter moon, and the constellation Scorpio danced at my right shoulder. Two boat lights twinkled on the dim line of the horizon, probably shrimpers, and illumination from South Padre Island glowed on my left. The road pointed directly into the eastern sky. Sharing this solitude with me was a long-legged, tailless, white-and-gray feral dog who politely came to the door of the car looking for a handout. His lack of fear was impressive, but he was not much interested in saltine crackers and shortly left to sniff the scattered trash cans along this largely undeveloped beach of Brazos Island State Recreation Area.

The sky changed quickly from black to indigo to muddy blue as the burnt orange sun emerged from the sea. When it freed itself from the horizon the sun became an oval of bright orange and then a circle of gold. There was no fog and the slanting light colored the sand to look like light brown sugar, gave mascara strokes to wind ripples in the beach, and draped long shadows on the cactus standing stiffly at attention behind the dunes. The grumbling, breaking waves momentarily held the angled light in green translucent curls that fell and dissolved into hissing foam upon the shore while a few early-rising gulls, sounding like big-city garbage collectors, noisily began their daily task of scavenging the frothy surf line. Dawn at the Boca Chica—many aspects were immemorial, dictated by nature; others were strongly influenced by human existence, as has been the world since the time of Adam and Eve.

The Texas coast is a part of a low plain, several hundred miles wide, that bands the United States from New York to Mexico. Not over 1,000 feet above the sea and submerged many times over geological time, the landform now gradually descends from the Balcones Escarpment in central Texas to the shore and then out into the Gulf of Mexico for six miles to form the Continental Shelf. The gentle topography produces slow meandering rivers and easy surf on the coastline.

Early settlers, buoyed on the tide of the American westward movement, sought the fertile soils, moderate temperatures, and generous rainfalls of the eastern Texas coastal plain and moved quickly inland to plant their cotton and corn. Understandably, during their rush the farmers and ranchers of the nineteenth century paid scant attention to the thin ribbon of sand that delimited water and land, or to the expansive salt marshes that often stood between the beaches and farming country. These areas were nonproductive for the Anglo settlers of the nineteenth century. At a time when human energy had to concentrate upon survival in the wilderness, the pioneers—Americans of all sorts, English, Irish, Czech, Africans, Germans, and others—sought out the good Texas soils. It was land so rich, according to talk, that a crop of ordinary white potatoes turned naturally into sweet potatoes. The beach and marsh were notably rejected and ignored.

Such rejection was not just a peculiarity of the settlers, either,

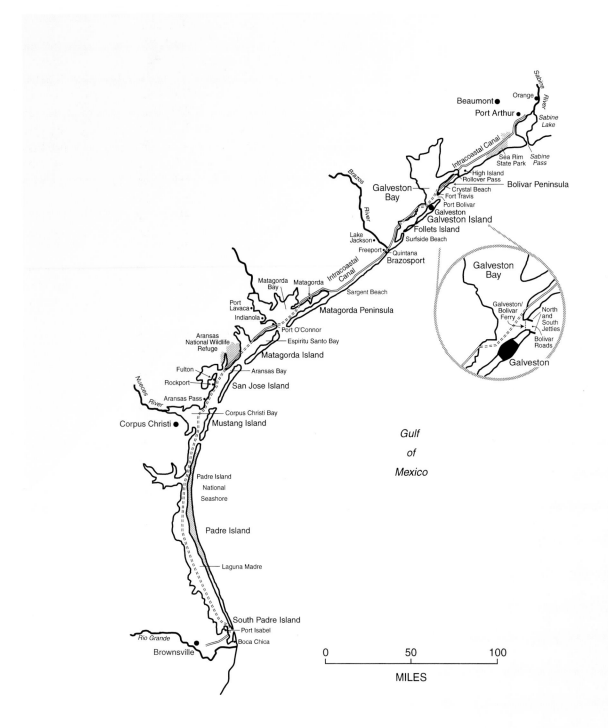

Beaumont

Orange

Sabine River

Port Arthur

Sabine Lake

Intracoastal Canal

Sea Rim State Park

Sabine Pass

Galveston Bay

High Island
Rollover Pass

Bolivar Peninsula

Brazos River

Crystal Beach
Fort Travis
Port Bolivar
Galveston
Galveston Island

Follets Island

Lake Jackson

Surfside Beach

Freeport

Quintana
Brazosport

Intracoastal Canal

Galveston Bay

Matagorda Bay

Matagorda

Sargent Beach

Galveston/
Bolivar Ferry

North
and
South
Jetties

Port Lavaca

Matagorda Peninsula

Bolivar
Roads

Indianola

Port O'Connor

Galveston

Aransas
National Wildlife
Refuge

Espiritu Santo Bay

Matagorda Island

Fulton

Aransas Bay

Rockport

San Jose Island

Nueces River

Aransas Pass

Corpus Christi Bay

Corpus Christi

Mustang Island

Gulf

of

Mexico

Padre Island

National

Seashore

Padre Island

Laguna Madre

South Padre Island

Port Isabel

Rio Grande

Boca Chica

Brownsville

0   50   100

MILES

because most Indians of Texas also shunned the shoreline. Two groups, among the poorest and least sophisticated of the natives, occupied the coast. To the east, from Galveston Bay into Louisiana, small, scattered bands of Atakapans hunted deer, raked in oysters, impaled flounders in shallow water, and gathered bird eggs for food. They poled crude blunt-end dugout canoes and speared alligators through the eyes to kill them. They extracted the ill-smelling body oil of the reptile to smear on themselves as mosquito repellent. The Atakapans wore little clothing, lived in crude brush huts, and, because of land conditions, engaged in no agriculture.[2] In general, they were peripheral to the more culturally complex Caddo Indians who lived to the north. Seemingly, these Atakapan Indians lived a marginal existence on land unwanted by more powerful groups, on land unable to support large numbers of people. Ominously, in the Choctaw language, their name meant "eaters of men."

From Galveston on toward Corpus Christi lived a similar group, the Karankawas. As with the Atakapans, knowledge about these Indians is limited, but they also apparently lived a nomadic life partly sustained by the coast. They fished the shallow lagoons in crude dugouts, made their pots leakproof with asphaltum that washed up on beaches, ate clams and oysters, and harvested the roots of cattails. The Karankawas possessed no agriculture of their own and moved periodically in search of a seasonal bounty from nature.[3] Noah Smithwick, when he arrived at Matagorda Bay in 1827, saw a band of Karankawas from the safety of a ship. "They were the most savage looking human beings I ever saw," he recorded. "Their ugly faces were rendered hideous by the alligator grease and dirt with which they were besmeared from head to foot as a defense against mosquitoes."[4] Smithwick, like other immigrants at the time, had no great liking of Indians and he was disappointed not to fire a cannon into their midst. His observations were tainted by prejudice, however, and the Atakapans and the Karankawas lived a successful hunting and gathering life on marginal land.

The difficulty with the coastal country was that it was not productive enough to sustain great numbers of people who only fished, hunted, and gathered food. Seasonally, after the spawning seasons of black drum and redfish during the fall and winter, the Karankawas broke into small bands and migrated inland to hunt bison and deer.[5] To be sure, the nearby marshes teemed with life. Snakes, alligators, birds in stunning variety, insects, small fish, larvae for oysters and shrimp were all a part of a salt wetland ecology now recognized for its importance. It was land difficult to hunt and impossible to farm, however, unless it was drained. That took capital, engineering, and great effort. In frontier Texas, where there existed cheap land that was easy for settlers to cultivate, why bother?

The small strip of sandy beach was even more difficult, for here was a desert environment in which only the most determined of plants and animals could survive. Texas beaches start near the Louisiana border at Sabine Pass and follow the 367-mile curving coastline southwestward to Mexico. They were formed, according to one explanation, by sand left behind when the sea level rose after the last ice age. Waves and currents, then, pushed the debris into islands. Another explanation is that wave action formed the islands and beaches from sand carried into the Gulf by rivers, including the Mississippi River. Gulf currents moving westward parallel to the mainland from the Mississippi dropped the particles, which then accumulated. Another powerful Gulf current swept northward along the coast of Mexico, performing the same beach-formation task. The streams met at Big Shell, midway on Padre Island, where the island curves eastward in one direction and southward in the other. Because of the turbulence of water and air, this has been a historic danger point for sailing ships, and a place of delight for people who collect sea shells.

From Galveston Bay to Mexico, the sandy beaches are found mainly on barrier islands. The islands vary in length and width and look fragile on a map. This somewhat belies their geologic assignment to protect the mainland from destructive hurricanes. Galveston Island, historically the most important, for example, is three miles wide and twenty-seven miles long. Padre Island, noted for contemporary tourist developments, is 130 miles long—

the longest sand-barrier island in the world. If given enough time and peace, live oak trees, sea oats, and morning glory vines grow to anchor the restless sand. However, the islands stand in harm's way. Unlike any other geographical point, where the sea meets the land there is constant combat.

Waves drop sand as they tumble ashore and in the washing movement push the grains first landward and then seaward. Sand does not stay in one place; it is in a dynamic environment. On land, if the sand grains escape the waves and tides, the water evaporates and the crystals become captives of the wind. They blow, often, into dunes which move slowly landward in the direction of the prevailing wind. Indeed, the whole sand-barrier island inches landward, as incipient islands form in the sandbars offshore. Storms may further the movement by washing the sand up and over to the bay side. It is debatable how far this can go, but Live Oak Ridge near Rockport is a stabilized Pleistocene Era sand-barrier island that is now part of the mainland.[6] The Bolivar Peninsula, moreover, is treated by the United States Corp of Engineers as a sand-barrier island even though it is attached to the mainland. It was once an island, apparently, and it has now become partially connected to the main shore.[7]

The wind, generally a strong offshore breeze whiffling in the ears, is a dominant weather feature. It not only dries the sand and creates its own sand sculptures, it also carries a heavy burden of humidity and salt. Like sea water, nature's ultimate solvent, the air possesses a corrosive quality. Houses almost always look tired and in need of a coat of paint; cars suffer premature rusting; women's hairdos, those with other than straight styling, demand frequent repair; and windows or eyeglasses exposed to the breeze require frequent washing. If the wind stops, as it does once in a while, armies of mosquitoes launch invasions from the nearby marshlands, but at dawn and dusk the wind rewards coastal residents with soft pastel skies of light blue, magenta, orange, and peach. Galveston writer Kate Cambridge commented in 1982, ". . . it's an evening sky again, that intermingled pink and blue, no, lavender, but yet there's all that gold . . . and if I could find a name for that color my own name would shine."[8]

At times the mainland and island chain is battered and rearranged by catastrophic storms, the worst of which are hurricanes. Warm, humid air rising from the mid-Atlantic Ocean creates the conditions for these swirling, broad storms that travel through the Caribbean and Gulf of Mexico and sometimes up the Atlantic seaboard during the months of June through November. Every other year, on average, they attack part of the Texas coastline with heavy rains, tornadoes, high tides, and counterclockwise winds blowing at more than seventy-three miles per hour.[9] When this happens, dunes are flattened, channels are opened through the islands, plants are uprooted, shorelines are changed, and a fresh layer of shell debris is scattered over the sand. Storm surges and flooding inflict most of this land damage, while wind and tornadoes strike at arrogant human structures. Even if a beach house survives a storm, the disconcerted owner may find that the beach line has shifted and that his prized vacation home now stands in the surf, or on prohibited state property. This creates a problem, because state law reserves the beach up to the vegetation line of the dunes for public use. Such is the difficulty when humans try to build their homes on moving islands of sand. Hurricanes, however, are a common occurrence and for the people who choose to defy them there can be no excuse.

To complicate matters, the sea level is rising. This has accelerated since the 1930s at a rate that amounts to one foot per century. Along the Texas coast, where there is a gentle slope, this can amount to 100 to 1,500 feet of beach per century. An estimate by one group of beach experts predicts, moreover, that in the twenty-first century, South Padre Island will shift 1,000 to 1,500 feet, Galveston Island, south of the seawall, from 1,000 to 2,000 feet, and Bolivar Peninsula from 500 to 1,000 feet. The evidence of movement is easy to see when the old oyster, snail, and clam shells from the inner lagoons turn up on the Gulf side as the sand rolls inland.[10] It is a shifting, dynamic environment.

Yet about nine percent of the Texas population live in the coastal counties, and large cities, including Brownsville, Corpus Christi, Houston, Galveston, Beaumont, and Port Arthur, are vulnerable to the reach of the great storms. There are ample reasons, however, for a choice of coastal location. The ports stand at a break in transportation, where items in transit must shift back and forth from ships to trucks, trains, airplanes, and even pipelines. In addition, fishers, including those in oyster and shrimp production, have a claim to the coast, as do off-shore oil companies sipping petroleum from the Continental Shelf. In times of warfare, reaching back to the Texas Revolution, and the War with Mexico, soldiers and sailors have made use of shoreline areas for bases of operation.

Beyond the economic and military purposes, there is another major reason for coastal habitation. Since 1920, tourists have sought recreation and entertainment from the seashore. Travelers, perhaps more than others, seek what is missing from their lives. From the seacoast, almost any seacoast, comes a faint call, a primordial voice that seems to beckon all human beings home. Roy Bedichek, one of Texas' most revered naturalists, heard this call and commented about his first boyhood trip to the beach at Galveston:

Upstate boys accustomed to playing about in the placid waters of ponds and inland streams here got the surprise of their lives. How well I remember the first rude embrace of the sea! With a number of companions far out on "West Beach," joyously naked, I rushed forward to meet the landward-racing waves. . . . I was knocked down, ducked, rolled, tossed about, strangled, until I learned to accommodate myself to the waves. Then came the thrill of being lifted, rocked, and gently wavering, like a falling leaf, let down, up and down again and again, in slow pulsative timing. I experienced with the whole body that original rhythm from which, some say, the very sense of rhythm in animal creation was derived, based back in the very beginning, before life left the sea.[11]

The seacoast is a reminder of faint connections, where the gentle surf of the Gulf of Mexico offers redemption to the spirit. The severe line of the horizon tolerates no trees, buildings, or telephone poles; it is an uncompromising border separating two enormous hemispheres of blue air and blue water. The endless roll of the waves indicates a power beyond human control—an unforgiving force that simply says, "I am not asking you, I am telling you." But the shore also carries the message, "I am, I have been, I will be, and you are a part of me." Somehow, a visit to the shore is both humbling and embracing at the same time. Although we of the human species crossed that desert barrier of surf and sand, we can still hear the voice of the ocean from our remote past.

This series of paintings and historical essays explores the Texas coast with an eye and a word for the human interaction at the shoreline. There are additional comments about plants, birds, and sea creatures, as well as ports, storms, cities, people, mineral wealth, recreation, and other topics. The book follows a simple geographical pattern, moving from Sea Rim Park and the Louisiana border to South Padre Island, close to the Boca Chica at the Mexican border. Both writing and painting are forms of art, and with this art we have hoped to provide an interpretation of the mythic and historical qualities of the seacoast of Texas.

THE SABINE CROSSING

The Sabine River basin has a troubled, uneasy history. Even today, Interstate 10 funnels travelers on viaducts over and across this haunted land in a hurried transit between Baton Rouge and Houston, seemingly to avoid disturbing questions. The southern part of Louisiana and southeastern Texas is swampy, and the name of the river course assigned by the early Spanish means "Cypress." It referred to the heavy, moss-covered, quietly oppressive cypress swamps of the lower river basin.

The Atakapan Indians who lived in the area at the time of European exploration roamed in family bands, the men hunting for deer and game, the women looking for wild potatoes. They scavenged this marginal land in order to live, smeared smelly alligator fat on their bodies to repel mosquitoes, and feared their stronger neighbors. The unit size of ten adults or so was dictated by the limits of food supply. Larger, more successful Indian groups occupied the better country to the north and practiced elementary agriculture. The weaker Atakapans could not compete, and a marooned French explorer witnessed their rough and cannibalistic ways.

François Simars de Bellisle sailed in August 1719 as a twenty-four-year-old ensign on a ship bound for Louisiana, but according to Bellisle the incompetent captain took them astray. When they reached Galveston Bay, Bellisle and four others went ashore in order to walk to the French colony. The ship was supposed to follow their campfires eastward along the shore, but by the second day the men on land noticed that the vessel had disappeared. Living thinly on deer and oysters, the group wandered the Indian trails from the Brazos River to the swamps of the Sabine, where they fell into mud up to their necks. His companions died of starvation, but Bellisle, turning back to the west, ran across some Atakapan Indians on a small island, gathering birds' eggs.

In wasted condition, the Frenchman, desperately looking for help, approached the Indians in a boat he had found. The Atakapans, however, noting his helpless condition, stole his equipment, including the boat, and stripped him of his clothes. They enslaved him, kept him naked, made him work about the campsites, and beat him occasionally, but gave him food—sometimes human flesh. As a joke, the Atakapans promised to deliver a letter for him to a "white man." With no particular destination, the letter passed as a curiosity from hand to hand among the tribes, but eventually it reached the French trading post at Natchitoches, Louisiana. The commandant, Louis Juchereau de Saint-Denis, sent friendly Hasinais Indians to retrieve the castaway. The Hasinais intimidated the Atakapans, rescued Bellisle, gave him a robe to wear, and escorted him to Natchitoches in April 1721.

En route, an intriguing Hasinai widow called Angelique nursed him back to full health and retained him for several months as a lover. Bellisle remained in the Louisiana colony until 1762 as a plantation owner, town official, and guide for various expeditions. One such expedition occurred in 1721, when he served as an interpreter for the La Harpe explorations of Galveston Bay. Bellisle's former captors were surprised and discomforted to see their slave return so soon and so well armed. They expected reprisals. As feared, nine of the Indians were taken captive to Biloxi—undoubtedly to Bellisle's pleasure—and from the captive group a vocabulary of the Atakapan language was extracted. The Indians shortly escaped, however. Bellisle eventually died in Paris in 1763.[1]

As Bellisle discovered, the lower Sabine area offered no land route into Louisiana. To the north, the Spanish and the French, however, pieced together a network of Indian trails with their own to form the Old San Antonio Road across Louisiana and Texas to the Rio Grande. It connected Natchitoches in Louisiana with Nacogdoches in Texas, and crossed the Sabine River at Gaines Ferry, some 125 miles from the coast. The road avoided the swampland and became a major route for heavy freight wagons and westward-moving pioneers burdened with slaves and household items. The ferry operated from 1797 until 1937, when it was finally replaced by a bridge. It crossed the river at the point of State Highway 21, now a part of the Toledo Bend Reservoir. The other major route into Texas was by sea, to ports at Galveston or Indianola. This sealane also avoided the swamps, but the Sabine River was not without merit or significance.

The river flows for 555 miles and drains a basin in Louisiana and Texas that has a rainfall of nearly fifty inches per year. This means that the river has the strongest flow of all Texas streams. It also means that there are floods—about every five years—on the flat coastal plain. Sabine Lake, fourteen miles long and seven wide, provides a salty tidal basin at the confluence of the Sabine and Neches rivers called Sabine Pass that reaches into the gulf. In the nineteenth century, small steamboats carrying supplies, people, and produce could chug through the pass upriver to the more secure locations. Thus, the upper Sabine basin was a location of choice for the Anglo-American pioneers and the shattered remnants of Indian tribes who were a part of the roiling westward movement of American civilization.

In 1803, the western boundary of the Louisiana Purchase was uncertain and the commanders in the field established a neutral strip to maintain peace between the United States and Spain. This hazy division ended in 1819 with the Adams-Onis Treaty that established the Sabine River as the boundary. Migrants forded the Sabine on their way into Texas, and during the Texas Revolution General Sam Houston and the Texas army retreated toward the river before the final stand at San Jacinto. General Antonio Lopez de Santa Anna, the Mexican dictator in pursuit, thought Houston was going to pass across the boundary to sanctuary in the United States. That did not happen, however. The Battle of San Jacinto was fought, and the Sabine River became the border between the United States and the Republic of Texas.

In September 1863, during the Civil War, General William B. Franklin led an army of Union soldiers on naval transports into Sabine Pass. The plan was to gain a foothold in Texas and capture the railroad that led to the city of Houston. To block such action, the Confederates built Fort Griffin, a dirt bastion with six cannons and some forty-three men. When the leading Yankee gunboats came within cannon range, the Rebels emerged from their shelters and opened fire. They disabled the *Sachem* with a shot to the boiler and clipped the tiller rope of the *Clifton*, causing it to run aground. The other two gunboats retired rather than face the rapid, accurate fire of the Confederate cannoneers. During the furious thirty-five-minute fight, the Rebel guns became so hot

that the barrels could not be touched until the next day. The entire invading army turned back. Sailors threw mules and supplies overboard to lighten their load and the humbled fleet returned to New Orleans. The Texas defenders captured the damaged gunboats and 315 prisoners in this so-called Battle of Sabine Pass.

When Lieutenant Henry C. Dane, the signal officer from the captured *Sachem*, met young Lieutenant Richard W. Dowling, who directed the Confederate batteries, he said, "And do you realize what you have done, sir?" When Dowling answered that he did not, Dane continued:

Well sir, you and your forty-three men, in your miserable little mud fort in the rushes, have captured two Yankee gunboats, carrying fourteen guns, a good number of prisoners, many stands of small arms and plenty of good ammunition. . . . And that is not the worst of your boyish tricks. You have sent three Yankee gunboats, 6,000 troops and a general out to sea in the dark. You ought to be ashamed of yourself, sir.[2]

Dowling, a handsome, reddish-haired Irishman, thus became a Texas hero. He continued to operate his popular saloon in Houston until 1867, when he died in a yellow-fever epidemic. In 1936, at the battle location, the state erected a statue to his memory, and in 1971 it purchased fifty-six acres to establish a state historical park, after the site almost became a garbage dump. Located fifteen miles south of Port Arthur off State Highway 87, the park today is a grassy respite from the surrounding boat facilities, rusting sheet metal warehouses, and an unused oil drilling platform resting along the Sabine Pass channel.

Farther down Highway 87 to the coast, the state purchased 15,000 acres with five miles of beachfront from an oil company to establish Sea Rim State Park in 1973. Its marshland protects alligators and migrating birds, while its Gulf beach is a home for endangered turtles and tourists. It is isolated, however. Highway 87, built in the 1930s, was a part of the "Hug-the-Coast" roadway system that was supposed to ring the Gulf coast and attract travelers. But tropical storms eroded the shore, and in 1983 Hurricane Alicia so undermined portions of the roadway that 320 feet of the

SABINE PASS

As one looks out over the calm serenity of Sabine Pass it is easy to forget that it has witnessed its share of turbulence, both natural and man-made. Storms have raged and done their worst, native Americans and explorers have left their footprints, and there was quite a skirmish here during the Civil War. The Texas Confederates captured over three hundred prisoners and sank two Union gunboats. It was an astonishing victory, considering the fact that there were only forty-three Confederates and six cannons in a miserable little mud fort on shore. The man who became a Texas hero that day was their leader, Dick Dowling.

Today that location is a state historical park which looks out over the pass to the lighthouse on the far shore. For many years the lighthouse guided ships to safe harbor in Texas, even though it stands on the Louisiana side of the pass. The lighthouse was built in 1856, was extinguished during the Civil War, and was afterwards relighted. The structure is most unusual, in that it is built of brick and is six-sided, with six large buttresses resembling a Jules Verne–style rocket ship.

The lighthouse, however, proved to be more than adequate, weathering many storms and hurricanes through the years. The other buildings did not fare so well, though, and today all that remains is the tower, silently poised above the boggy marshland.

The future of this corner of Texas was assured by the discovery of oil in 1901, and the city of Port Arthur prospered from the export of petroleum products, especially during World War II. Of course, the oil and chemical plants caused much pollution in the area. However, those in control of the petrochemical plants are beginning to be aware of their impact on the environment, and the quality of the air and water is showing signs of recovery. Fishing is a reality once again in Sabine Pass, but the remnants of the oil boom are very visible, in the form of an abandoned oil rig just off the shore of the historical park. Oil put this part of Texas on the map, but it almost killed it as well.

THE SABINE HOTEL—PORT ARTHUR

In 1895 Arthur E. Stilwell purchased 53,000 acres of land in Jefferson County to serve as the terminus and port for his railroad, the Kansas City, Pittsburgh and Gulf. This was the beginning of Port Arthur. Mr. Stilwell realized that prospective settlers and businessmen coming to the city would need a pleasant place to stay, and so in 1896 he began work on the beautiful Victorian-style Sabine Hotel. He located it on a low bluff overlooking Lake Sabine and built a quarter-mile-long pleasure pier over the water. The seventy-room hotel was set in the middle of a beautiful park filled with rare tropical plants, and the hotel, park, and pier were all illuminated by arc and incandescent lights.

Not long after the hotel was completed a storm blew in, flooding the city streets with water five feet deep. Hogs, cattle, alligators, and snakes were seen swimming for high ground. Awakened by the screaming wind, some of the residents formed a human chain and, aiding one another, made their way to the Sabine Hotel. Water stood two feet deep on the first floor and the employees had covered the windows with furniture and bedding. The hotel was well built and withstood the wind and water, and all who sought shelter there survived the storm to return and rebuild or repair their homes.

Unfortunately, this beautiful hotel was barely seven years old when a fire broke out in the kitchen on July 17, 1903. It was discovered early and was thought to be under control. However, the second-hand fire engine which had recently been purchased broke down, rendering the fire department helpless. The people watched with dismay as this beautiful Victorian hotel burned to the ground.

380-foot right-of-way sank into the Gulf of Mexico. The Highway Department closed the road from Sea Rim to High Island in a rare concession to the power of nature. There is no plan to revive the "Hug-the-Coast" concept. Sea Rim State Park, with its un-shaded sand, dunes, and salt marsh, therefore, remains quietly at the end of the road—a difficult place for casual tourists, a good spot for alligators, birds, turtles, and people seeking solitude.[3]

Significant in the history of the area, also, was the development of Port Arthur, the only town that began through the advice of brownies, or fairies. Arthur Stilwell, a man who wrote plays, poetry, songs, and novels, was also a railroad magnate who took the advice of brownies. He claimed they spoke to him while he slept. He wanted a Gulf port for his southward-building railway, the Kansas City, Pittsburg, and Gulf (KCPG, commonly known as the Pee Gee). Other railroads utilized Galveston, but Stilwell had a dream in which a voice instructed him, "Locate your terminal city on the north shore of Sabine Lake . . . for Galveston will some day be destroyed." He established the town as advised in 1895 and proceeded to build docks and a ship channel. Stilwell envisioned that swampy Port Arthur would also become a destination for tourists, even though his workmen had to wear double shirts and pants as armor against the mosquitoes. The ethereal advice was correct about Galveston, but Stilwell, nonetheless, lost control of the enterprise by the end of the century to promoter and investor John W. Gates.[4]

The brownies, moreover, failed to predict the gusher at Spindletop which pushed Texas to the forefront of the oil industry. Pipelines snaked onto the Port Arthur docks and oil companies erected storage tanks at Sabine Pass. Stilwell's town might have had a serious rival with the city of Sabine Pass, but the howling winds and slanting rain of the four-day 1915 hurricane persuaded the oil companies to move inland. Sabine Pass declined as a result of the storm and Port Arthur endured by constructing elaborate levees. Port Arthur became an oil town and lost its tourism ambitions. During World War II, along with nearby Orange, the city became a temporary shipbuilding site. Following the war, with a "Petrochemical Row" of refineries on its northeastern border, Port Arthur bragged, "We Oil the World."

The price was an overwhelming odor of oil in the air, a lung-cancer rate in Jefferson County that was 20 percent higher than in the rest of the nation, a lead content in the water supply that was five times higher than was considered safe, a lakefront that became barren of fish due to chemical pollution, and the slow death of the downtown shopping district. The integration of schools was blamed for a white flight to the north, and the oil depression of the 1980s was a cause for unemployment in the petrochemical industry. Downtown business people fled to the malls along the six-lane highways that looped to the north and streaked toward Beaumont. Only beer joints and pawn shops remained behind as a residue in the disintegrating downtown area. Today, security bars placed over residential and business windows testify to the the physical danger of the old area. It is understandable that Janis Joplin, arguably the greatest white blues singer in American history, came out of the Port Arthur environment with its depressed, disordered history. There have been some efforts by politicians to redirect Port Arthur in order to fulfill Stilwell's dream of tourism, but as a construction company owner commented in 1983, "This town is a six-pack of beer and television, blue-collar town."[5] It seems unlikely to change.

When the historical accounts are put together, the lower Sabine River proves to be a difficult and negative land. The Atakapan Indians lived a marginal life; the Civil War brought glorious victory to one side, ignominy to the other, and no change in the outcome of the war; hurricanes have punished roads, businesses, and people; the petrochemical industry has aided the economy, but exacted a human and ecological price; a port city has lost cohesion and direction. The salt flats and cypress swamps have been inhospitable obstacles for human habitation. Isolated Sea Rim Park—a place to visit, but not to live in—is a symbol of this tortured land.

THE BOLIVAR PENINSULA

racing the Gulf shore of Sea Rim Park near Port Arthur is a beach that extends southwestward along the length of the Bolivar peninsula. It once served as a road for people traveling to Sabine Pass. After a portion of the highway from Port Arthur washed away in the storms of 1980 and 1983, the state closed the road and refused to rebuild it. Maintaining the pavement was too expensive and once more the beach is the pathway into this isolated region. Much of this coastal land is a wildlife refuge and unsuitable for residential development. Highway 124 from Beaumont, Winnie, and Stovall connects again with the severed Highway 87 at High Island, a village near the base of the peninsula and close to the sea.

The village was well named. Thirty-eight feet above sea level atop a salt dome, it is the highest point on the Gulf of Mexico between Mobile, Alabama and the Yucatan of Mexico. It is thickly covered with live oak trees, has a view of the Gulf, and in hurricanes has often been the only land above water—a high island. Historically, during such storms on this part of the Gulf coast, some of the safer places have been among its trees. Shaped by the constant offshore sea breeze, other trees close to the shore point with leafy arms to the live oaks on the higher ground as if in warning.

The peninsula, named by early nineteenth-century pirates or explorers for Simon Bolivar, the great South American liberator, reaches southwestward into the sea for twenty-seven miles like a sun-bleached finger bone. It is no more than three miles wide. East Bay, part of Galveston Bay, along with Galveston Bay itself, borders the north side. This side of the peninsula is pierced by the Intracoastal Waterway, a barge canal built in the 1930s and important for water transportation during World War II. Although disturbed by barge traffic, the salt marshes of these nearby bays have long been prime habitat for ducks and alligators. Forest McNeir, who grew up in the East Bay during the late nineteenth century, lived by his skill with a shotgun. He sold alligator hides for sixty cents and mallards for twenty cents, and claimed that he once killed thirty-five teal ducks with a single shot as they rested on a reef. Ducks were sometimes so thick in the bay areas that he said he could not see the water. Putting on shoes to make a proper appearance, McNeir would transport his game, as well as melons from Bolivar farmers, in a small sailboat to market at Galveston across the bay.[1]

Occupation of the peninsula began in 1816, when soldiers of fortune following Francisco Xavier Mina built an earthwork fort at the tip. Mina's filibuster into Spanish Mexico failed and the fort deteriorated. Ambitious James Long, however, rebuilt the structure in 1820, and the next year left his wife, child, and a black servant girl there while he went off on his own ill-fated adventure of revolution. Jane Long, pregnant and loyal, stubbornly waited, but her husband never returned. He was killed in Mexico City. Others at the fort left, and after a hard, cold winter, Jane Long, "the Mother of Texas," moved with settlers up the San Jacinto River. Permanent settlement on the peninsula began in 1838 after the Texas Revolution, when Samuel D. Parr, an Englishman, claimed a league of land. Farmers slowly followed in order to raise cattle, watermelons, cabbages, beans, and cantaloupe on the fertile land behind the dunes for markets in Beaumont and Galveston. They learned to fight off the squadrons of swamp mosquitoes by attaching screen wire to their hats, and by 1885 there were 500 people living on the peninsula.[2]

Point Bolivar, the tip of the peninsula, had become important by this time. It marked the point of entrance into Galveston Bay and was the closest segment of the peninsula to the thriving port of Galveston, three miles away. It was an easy place for ships to go aground, however, and as early as 1831 several travelers erected a driftwood spar with a red-and-white flag on the tip as a warning for sailors. Groundings on the sandbars continued, however, and in 1852 the United States government built a 76-foot lighthouse on the point. Cast-iron sections were added six years later and the height raised to one hundred feet. Rebel soldiers, fearing that the light would aid the Yankee blockade, tore it down during the Civil War, but the federal government built another one in 1872. The new lighthouse was 117 feet high, constructed of riveted iron plates, brick, and concrete, boldly painted with five broad, horizontal black-and-white bands, and topped with a powerful revolving beacon. After improvements, its beam could be seen seventeen miles out at sea.[3]

The lighthouse served as a refuge during hurricanes, and continued its faithful service until 1933, when it was replaced by better navigational devices. Up until then, neighbors in the dark of night counted upon the slow rotation of the light that appeared every fifteen seconds. "It was bright, bright, bright," said Anne B. Mouton, whose family arrived at Bolivar in 1928. They depended upon kerosene lamps in their home, but used an outside shower room. "If we had to go out and get a bucket of water or use the restroom, we'd wait till the light came," she explained. "The light turned slow—if we'd wait a minute, it would come again, you know. We depended on that light, and we hated it when they cut it off." The government sold the lighthouse in 1947 and it passed into private hands. Today, it still stands as a romantic landmark, a rusting sentinel with its duty over, a nostalgic reminder of an earlier era.[4]

Also at Point Bolivar are the remnants of Fort Travis, built on the site of James Long's post, where he left his pregnant wife and child. Construction of the fort began in 1898 as a part of the coastal defense system, and it eventually included barracks, gun emplacements, and a sea wall. It was used in both world wars, provided shelter during hurricanes, and, after passing through private hands, became a county park in 1973. Close by, the federal government also constructed the north jetty, a pink granite stone wall standing several feet above the surface of the water and extending five miles southeastward into the Gulf of Mexico. Completed in 1896, the north jetty, along with a twin constructed off the tip of Galveston Island, redirected bay currents to scour a ship channel into Galveston Bay.[5] The jetty system, identified by lighthouses, made Galveston a deep-water port, gave access to the Houston Ship Channel built in 1914, and created dreams for the citizens of Point Bolivar.

To them, Galveston was host to blue-water vessels, so why not Bolivar? In March 1896, to the accompaniment of a whistle, a bell, and a long-winded speech by the subcontractor, the Gulf and Interstate Railway from Beaumont via High Island puffed to the point. The line shortly fell into financial trouble, and it was taken over by Abel Head "Shanghai" Pierce, the legendary cattle baron from Wharton and Matagorda counties. Meanwhile, grower W. C. Patton shipped out a carload of watermelons, land developers promoted the inland town of Winnie, and Charles Taylor Cade built the Sea View Hotel at High Island. Bolivar was on the move.

In 1897, Cade, a cattle rancher from New Iberia, Louisiana, shipped in a load of cypress over the G&I (popularly known as the Gee Ni) and constructed his three-story Sea View Hotel on the hill at High Island overlooking the Gulf. It had a large dining and dancing room on the first floor, bedrooms on the second and third floors, and an observation cupola on top. Guests were met by horse and wagon at the train stop, and they could ride a private horse-drawn trolley to the beach for swimming or dancing in a screened pavilion. It was the beginning of tourism on the Bolivar Peninsula.

The railroad gave access to the beaches and offered a one-dollar excursion rate from Beaumont. Other resorts and hotels popped up along the right-of-way. At Patton, now Crystal Beach, halfway down the peninsula, Charles Patton built a hotel with a pavilion and bathhouse extending over the water. It was lighted for night swimming and equipped with ropes to steady the bathers as they ventured into the pulsing surf. In a day when women's swimming costumes were made of heavy wool that covered them from ankle to elbow, and when most people could not swim, ropes were a necessary precaution.[6]

This blossoming tourist business, along with other plans for development, came to a sobering halt, however, after two destructive hurricanes fifteen years apart. In September 1900 a medium-to-large-sized hurricane crashed ashore at Bolivar and Galveston. The new weather station at Galveston issued some warning, but no one realized how bad it would be. There were gusts of 120 miles per hour and a storm surge of fifteen feet. Water flowed over the Bolivar Peninsula, which was only four to eight feet above sea level. The G&I excursion train was marooned at the Patton station in the screaming wind, with waves crashing against the cars. The tide surged over the top of the dance pavilion and the town washed away.

At Point Bolivar, some 120 refugees huddled in the lighthouse, sitting two-by-two on the inside spiral staircase. Seeking fresh rain water caught in a bucket at the top, they found it salty with sea spray. Only the lighthouse and the keeper's residence were spared; the new fort was wrecked and eleven soldiers drowned. At High Island, houses, the railroad, and the Sea View Hotel survived. An estimated forty-one people died on the peninsula, with livestock, houses, boats, crops, and railway washed away. "Shanghai" Pierce lost about $1.25 million to the storm. The Gulf and Interstate Railway was a wreck, with 25 miles of track uprooted, 100 cars turned over, and five engines left upside down. "I won't rebuild the Gulf and Interstate," he said with disgust. "If the state wants the charter they can have it back. I am done with that road and that is all there is to it. If anyone else wants to go in there and rebuild, let them do it."[7]

Rebuilding did take place. People picked up driftwood to construct new dwellings; they buried the bodies that washed up on the beaches; they replanted their farms. The G&I reverted to its original owners, who dug the equipment out of the sand and restored it to operating condition. Passengers of its interrupted last run in 1900 were given free rides in 1903. L. P. Featherstone, a former congressman from Arkansas who directed the line, was an optimist, and a dreamer. He bought 2,500 acres at Point Bolivar and platted a new town. He was able to persuade Congress to dredge a deep-water channel to his dock and he turned the G&I over to the Santa Fe Railroad. Featherstone arranged a contract with Bethlehem Steel to ship iron ore from mines around Longview through Port Bolivar to Philadelphia, and the Santa Fe constructed an impressive ore dock 325 feet long and 58 feet high. Featherstone endured the small hurricane of 1909 and promoted his "Brooklyn of Galveston Harbor," as he called it in brochures. After several ore shipments, however, investment and cargos faltered with the uncertainties of World War I in Europe. At this critical juncture, the sea once more hammered the peninsula.

This time there was more advance notice. Rockets from the weather bureau at Galveston warned ships of the coming hurricane, while engineers on the train from Beaumont spread the alarm and picked up people to carry them out of the way. Some sixty people huddled in the Point Bolivar lighthouse, sitting once more two-by-two on the cold iron steps. This storm, however, was stronger than the one fifteen years earlier. Gusts reached 125 miles per hour and the iron tower wobbled twelve inches at the top. The assistant keeper, J. P. Brooks, noted that the iron structure "shook and swayed in the wind like a giant reed." The rotation mechanism of the light broke, and an iron door at the base of the lighthouse blew open. Brooks, with a line tied to his waist, ventured outside to secure the door before wind and swirling water could erode the inside foundation of the lighthouse. He succeeded in closing it, but returned bruised and battered. The next afternoon, as the storm waters drained away, it became clear to the refugees that once more a hurricane had destroyed Point Bolivar.[8]

The 1915 hurricane killed an estimated forty-two people and left the peninsula a watery wasteland. Some people who failed to escape by train to the crowded hotels of Beaumont survived by clinging to the oak trees near High Island and along the ridges. The Sea View Hotel, along with a few other houses, managed to weather the storm, but the railroad was once more devastated. Again it was rebuilt and managed to continue operation until 1942, but the grand plans of Featherstone did not survive.[9] The storm of 1915, seemingly, drained the entrepreneurial spirit out of the peninsula. The ore fields gave out and other ports, such as Houston, rose to prominence.

Still, the raw attraction of a barrier island remained. William D. Gordon of Beaumont, who owned an orange grove and house at the village of Caplen, inspected his property two weeks after the 1915 storm. The grove was beaten down, but his house, called "The Breakers," suffered only minor damage. Gordon still hoped to enjoy his summer vacation on the peninsula and commented, "The beach is very expansive and more beautiful than ever before."[10]

What endured on the Bolivar Peninsula was this attraction of the beach and an opportunity for recreation. The bright sunlit sand peninsula became a place for small vacation homes, a spot to fish, a destination for students during their spring break from studies, and a location for rowdy people to celebrate Independence Day with little restriction. At Rollover, where the distance between the Gulf and the bay was only about one-quarter mile, the Texas Game and Fish Commission cut a small channel in 1955 and established a small park. The canal served as a route for spawning fish and has become an easily accessible fishing "hole" abundant with croakers, trout, redfish, and flounders. Rollover, supposedly, was a point for the transfer of contraband items, including prohibition-day liquor, from the Gulf to East Bay. Moreover, since the Texas coast was on a major flyway for migrating birds, ecotourists have flocked to the peninsula in the last half-century.[11] In 1994 some 179 species of birds were counted, including the piping plover, which was on the endangered list.[12] Thus, there was ample reason for vacationers to visit Bolivar.

Crystal Beach, the only town that was incorporated, experienced a boom. Unlike most of the peninsula, this place benefited from beach accretion, due to the sand-collecting effects of the north jetty. In five years' time, during the last years of the 1950s, Crystal Beach boomed from five homes to six hundred houses. Although it became the most populated town on the peninsula, with a population estimated currently at 1,600, it also was estimated that eighty percent were only weekend residents.[13] Local government was expensive and a bother, so the citizens of Crystal Beach voted to disincorporate and revert to county control in 1987. After a fight, the vote was reconfirmed in 1989.[14]

With the exception of ranching and some oil wells on the salt dome at High Island, the peninsula thereby became a vacation area—a place to visit, but certainly not a place for permanent residence. Most of the vacation homes, standing on stilts over the low sand, are not expensive. They appear fragile and expendable, as if the builders knew they were only temporary. The scars of past storms can be readily seen and future hurricanes are to be expected. In October and November 1996 storms with high tides washed away twenty-five to fifty feet of beach near Rollover Pass. Two homes were lost and fifty others damaged. Governor George W. Bush declared Bolivar a disaster area and the state placed 2,700 hay bales along the beach to help rebuild the lost dunes.[15] Here, perhaps, the lesson of the barrier islands has been learned: Thou shalt not build your house upon a foundation of sand.

(PRECEDING PAGE)

THE BOLIVAR LIGHTHOUSE

Since 1852 there has been a light at this spot on Point Bolivar, guiding ships through the narrow channel to Galveston Bay and sheltering refugees from the storms. The Civil War saw the cast-iron lighthouse dismantled by the Confederates and probably used in the war effort. By 1872, a 116-foot lighthouse, much taller than its predecessor, was constructed of brick and cast-iron sheets. For a while the lighthouse was painted red, but later it was repainted in black and white stripes.

The 1900 hurricane, which nearly devastated Galveston, only inflicted minor damage on the lighthouse, while the keeper saved 125 people, lodged and fed them on the station, and exhausted the month's supply of food he had just purchased. Fifteen years later, another hurricane caused considerable damage, carrying away the oil house and leaving the keeper with only two gallons of oil with which to keep the light going. The keeper reportedly turned the revolving machinery by hand all night in an effort to conserve his last two gallons of oil, and guided vessels to safety through the storm. During this storm, sixty people sought refuge on the steps of the lighthouse, the only place on the peninsula that remained above water.

Decommissioned by the Lighthouse Service in 1933, the darkened Bolivar lighthouse is lovingly cared for today by private citizens who use it as their summer retreat. But as one crosses on the ferry from Galveston to Bolivar Peninsula through the choppy waters, dodging the ocean-going vessels, one might remember with gratitude the lighthouse that enabled so many ships to make safe passage to harbor.

GALVESTON ISLAND

*B*olivar has always existed in the mythic shadow of Galveston. From Point Bolivar, where Highway 87 is interrupted by Bolivar Roads, the water course leading into the bay, Galveston Island is easily seen only three miles away. There was once talk about building a high bridge, but it was too expensive, given the amount of traffic. Instead, the Texas Department of Transportation maintains a twenty-four-hour ferry service for travelers. Attended by raucous squadrons of acrobatic, black-headed laughing gulls, the fifteen-minute ride, along with the view, provides one of the more memorable free delights for a tourist in Texas. It also serves as a dramatic introduction to Galveston, an island and city unique in the history of the state.

Like the Bolivar Peninsula, Galveston Island is twenty-seven miles long and about three miles wide. It is a true sand island. Once in 1891, when people were drilling for fresh water, the drill went 1,500 feet deep through various layers of sand, clay, shell, and sandstone and pushed up fragments of wood from 900 feet, but no water. It really was an island of sand, and fresh water had to be piped from the mainland or captured in cisterns from rainfall. An unbroken beach of brown-sugar-like, beige-colored sand distinguishes the Gulf side. The beach has grown into a broad expanse on the lee side of the south jetty, and diminished somewhat on the more westerly portions. Since the 1840s, residents have planted oleanders that bloom red, yellow, pink, salmon, and white. There are some sixty varieties of these shrubs. With its palm trees that give the island a tropical look and its houses on stilts, Galveston has long impressed visitors and residents as being different from the rest of Texas. And, it is.

It was on the Galveston beach, probably, that Cabeza de Vaca, an ill-starred Spanish explorer, and his men were marooned in 1528. They were at first aided by local Karankawa Indians who were hunting and fishing on the island. The Indians even wept in sympathy for thirty minutes at the plight of the naked white strangers. Later, when the natives began to die, from what was presumed to be a European disease, de Vaca and the others were enslaved. After six years he escaped, and lived to write the first description of the land that became the American Southwest. De Vaca held no great affection for Galveston and referred to it as the "Island of Doom." Later visitors with better luck, however, were enchanted by the beach. Even the censorious Francis C. Sheridan, a young Irishman in the British diplomatic service of the 1830s who hated the City of Galveston, praised the beach, that he claimed had the "whitest, firmist, & most beautiful sand I ever saw."[1]

The other side of the island consists of serrated mud flats and salt marshes facing a similar mainland two miles distant across the shallow water of West Bay, an extension of Galveston Bay. This unattractive landward side, however, possessed an unusual geographic feature that determined the history of the city that grew up on the eastern end of the island. The natural tidal currents of Galveston Bay scooped out a harbor that was, historically, the best landing point between New Orleans and Veracruz. Its usefulness was first discovered by pirates and revolutionaries in 1816. Don Louis Aury, appointed commodore of the navy of Mexico by Mexican patriots and rebels in New Orleans, established a base at Galveston in order to raid Spanish shipping. In 1817 he carried the invading army of Henry Perry and Xavier Mina to capture the Spanish town of Soto La Marina, then quarreled with the leaders and returned to his base.

During Aury's absence the deposed pirate of Barataria Bay in Louisiana, Jean Laffite, took over the harbor. Aury moved on to the coast of Florida while Laffite established an outlaw town of 1,000 people and profited as a broker for buccaneers. In turn, the United States Navy forced Laffite to abandon his nest in 1821 and Galveston Island fell into the hands of the Republic of Mexico. During the Texas Revolution the island became a refuge for the retreating Texas government, and then became a part of the Republic of Texas. Shortly thereafter, in 1838, ten associates led by Michel B. Menard bought the land at the northeastern tip and established the City of Galveston. Its main asset was the superior natural harbor on the bay side.

The city grew as the major port for nineteenth-century Texas. It was a place where trade goods were transferred back and forth between small river steamships and oceangoing ships. Cotton,

OLEANDERS

Oleanders may have originated as far away as the Golan Heights in Israel, where they still grow. They were taken to Spain and from there they were imported to Galveston in buckets aboard a trading schooner by Joseph Osterman. When he reached Galveston in 1841 he gave some of the plants to his sister, Mrs. Isadore Dyer, who in turn shared cuttings with her neighbors. The plants adapted well and grew profusely, so that today the streets and gardens of Galveston are aglow with color from May to September and visitors are astounded by their beauty.

The original plants were pink and white, but from those some thirty-two varieties have been developed, ranging in color from white to yellow, pale pink, salmon, and deep rose red. They are found with single, double, and even triple petals. The plants seem to thrive in the salt-laden soil and air of the coast.

Many legends about the oleander have been written, among them stories about princesses, villains, Greek gods, and a mother whose prayers to St. Joseph for her sick child were answered.

Although Galveston was probably the first to grow oleanders and has become known as "the oleander city," they beautify the entire Gulf coast, from the Sabine river to the Rio Grande.

deer hides, sugar, molasses, and pecans arrived at the Galveston docks from the mainland, where this produce of the countryside was traded for urban manufactured products—books, clothing, coffee, nails, gunpowder, and so forth. Since the port was on an island, small steamboats puffing black smoke and sparks carried the trade items through Galveston Bay and up Buffalo Bayou to Houston, where they were transferred to ox wagons destined for the interior of Texas. Galveston flourished with its cotton factors, financial strength, and access to the sea. It was the largest city in Texas, according to the federal census, with 14,000 people in 1870 and 22,000 in 1880. It survived the Civil War, when the port was practically abandoned, then recovered, made money from the occupation by northern troops during reconstruction, and endured periodic yellow-fever epidemics. Decline began again, however, with the building of transcontinental rail systems that siphoned off trade, and with the construction of rival man-made ports. Moreover, the Texas oil boom of the early twentieth century bypassed the island.

There was another major difficulty—the hurricane of 1900. It was the same storm that submerged the Bolivar Peninsula, sent refugees to the stairwell of the lighthouse, and destroyed the new railroad. At Galveston its devastation was worse. In fact, it was the worst natural disaster in terms of mortality in the history of the United States. About 6,000 people died. Interestingly, there was some warning of the coming tempest; it was not a surprise. Isaac M. Cline, the resident climatologist of the new U.S. Weather Service, guessed from the long swells breaking on the sand that a hurricane noted in Florida and then lost in the Gulf was about to come ashore at Galveston. He took his horse and buggy to warn people along the beach, sent the dreaded red-and-black-square hurricane flags snapping up the flagpoles in the growing wind, and gathered neighbors into his specially designed storm-proof home. Galveston Island was no higher than the Bolivar Peninsula—about eight-and-a-half feet at most—and was vulnerable.

The hurricane roared ashore on September 8, 1900. It flooded the island with a storm surge of water fourteen-and-a-half feet deep, which left the wooden-block streets bobbing in the water. It uprooted a trolley line along the beach, and in the tumbling water the rails fastened to wooden ties became a destructive scythe. Cline's house was undercut and the house rolled on its side. The climatologist's brother, clutching a child, jumped into the churning waves from a window, but the others in the house, some fifty people, were trapped in the timbers as they gurgled and swirled underwater. Cline managed to gasp to the surface, found his brother and other children, and endured the night on floating debris. With planks at their backs the men protected themselves and the youngsters from the pieces of black roof slate sent slicing through the air by the wind.

The Clines huddled on a pile of urban wreckage until the storm abated, and looked with disbelief at the havoc in the calm, moist sunlight of the morning. The hurricane had destroyed about one-third of the city. Six blocks of houses along the shoreline had been swept up into a tall, long debris pile that stretched through the city like a high-tide line. Bodies of humans, pets, cattle, horses, mules, starting to decay, were mingled among the boards, timbers, roofing, and litter of city life. The sixteen ships that had been in the harbor were scattered and aground. Officials and townspeople, however, quickly organized cleanup operations, restored water supply and other utilities, and cremated the bodies. The national guard suppressed looting, and in mid-October Galveston cotton merchants sent a record shipment through the port.

Important in the recovery was the development of community cooperation, called "the Galveston spirit," that included a fierce determination to remain on the island. Citizens could have abandoned the city site, as the people of Indianola had done fourteen years earlier, and indeed about 2,000 people moved from Galveston. The majority, however, stubbornly remained and took action to protect themselves from future assaults of the sea. They erected a concrete seventeen-foot seawall along the Gulf side, designed by the former head of the Corps of Engineers, General Henry M. Robert. Eventually, with extensions, it reached ten miles and became the largest and most successful seawall of any barrier island in the world.[2] To make sure it stayed in place, engineers raised the elevation of the island by pumping sand under jacked up homes and buildings. The island's new elevation began at the top of the seawall and sloped to the bay side. The citizens also built an all-weather concrete bridge to the mainland to assure a secure means of escape in times of trouble. All of this took time, innovative effort, and money. To oversee the extensive construction, the Galveston elite inaugurated a new type of city government—the commission form, which inspired national emulation and lasted in Galveston from one year after the disaster until 1960.

Following this cataclysm, Galveston's population and business grew slowly compared with the rest of Texas. The city was already in decline from the economic effects of railroads and rival ports, but another event, ill-timed for Galveston, sealed its fate. The Texas oil bonanza, introduced by the dramatic gusher at Spindletop near Beaumont in 1901, began at the time that Galveston was struggling for its redemption. This new source of wealth bypassed the Island City. Oil pipelines snaked into Beaumont, Port Arthur, and Houston. Companies constructed their refineries at safer inland points, such as the Houston Ship Channel, or between Port Arthur and Orange in Southeast Texas. The management headquarters of the oil companies gravitated to Houston, and that former servant of Galveston started its rise to become the fourth largest city in the United States. Galveston would become Houston's playground.

On the island, meanwhile, using their energy and money, the residents focused upon constructing the defenses against the sea that would ensure their survival. Their plans succeeded. In 1915, Galvestonians crouched behind their wall and watched their concrete shield stop the fury of a major hurricane. The concave face of the seawall deflected the heavy waves upward and dissipated their force into splash and spray. There was flooding, but only five people died and Galveston telegraphed its triumph to the world. In the following century, the most secure place on the island during the periodic hurricanes was behind the Galveston seawall. It still is, but the seventeen-foot wall is yet to be tested by an extreme storm surge like that of Hurricane Carla, which reached twenty-two feet in Lavaca Bay in 1961, or that of Hurricane Camille, which struck Mississippi in 1969 with twenty-two-and-a-half feet. The Galveston defenses, nevertheless, were a technological victory for the Island City, a successful conquest over nature by engineering and determination. They were the best yet devised for a sand-barrier island.

Other Texas cities, however, competed with Galveston for economic power and population. A group of developers from Duluth, Minnesota, starting in 1893, dredged a deep-water channel at the tip of the mainland northwest of Galveston Island and established Texas City as another port on Galveston Bay. This was the place that in 1947 suffered one of the worst peacetime explosions in history, when two vessels carrying ammonium nitrate caught fire and blew up. The blast destroyed the docks and killed almost 600 people.

On the island, although the cotton exports remained and the University of Texas Medical School expanded, the city's growth stalled at the level of a mid-sized town. The population totals actually declined in the 1960s, and they remained around 60,000 for the rest of the century. Galveston, however, transformed itself into the most significant tourist city in Texas. This remarkable change involved two major phases, conveniently divided at mid-century.

In the first half of the century the city became infamous with a trident of sin—gambling, illegal liquor, and prostitution. Following the Civil War, the recovering town was overrun with virile, young Northern soldiers, and a red-light area of saloons, bagnios, and variety theaters (the nineteenth-century equivalent of a burlesque theater) developed along and around Postoffice Street near the port. The industry was run by individual madams—regulated, but not suppressed by the police; and tolerated by the community. This infamous red-light area, probably the most notorious in Texas, remained in operation through the Great Depression and both world wars. Considering the number of prostitutes per capita—a ratio of 1:62, compared with 1:130 in Shanghai in the 1930s—Galveston's Postoffice Street was world class.

JEAN LAFFITE'S CAMPECHE

While the pirate Jean Laffite's exploits in Louisiana are very well documented, since he lived there for many years, the opposite is true of his stay in Galveston. We do know that when his band was expelled from Louisiana he set up a new headquarters on the island of Galveston. He called it "Campeche," and it was located on the bay side of the island at about the location of present-day Eleventh Street. An eyewitness reported many years later that the only house in the camp belonged to Laffite. It was two stories high, was called "Maison Rouge" (red house) because it was painted red (no one knows why), and was fronted by two cannons. The crude huts of Laffite's men and their families surrounded Maison Rouge. After only a few years he was again asked to move on by the U.S. Government. From this time on the movements of Jean Laffite are lost to recorded history, but many legends of him abound along the Gulf coast, even as far away as the Yucatan, and fortune hunters have, to no avail, dug for his treasure that is said to be buried somewhere on the coastal islands.

HOLD ON TO YOUR FAITH, BUT RESPECT THE FAITH OF OTHERS

Galveston has one of the finest collections of nineteenth-century buildings still existing in the United States today, due in no small measure to the talents of architect Nicholas Joseph Clayton. Mr. Clayton came to Galveston in 1873 as supervising architect for the building of the Tremont Hotel and the First Presbyterian Church. He remained in Galveston the rest of his life, designing and building many of this city's palatial homes, public buildings, and churches. Because he was a deeply religious man, his favorite projects were the churches, which he designed not only in Galveston but throughout Texas and the rest of the United States. Among the churches of Galveston he either designed or made renovations and additions to are the First Presbyterian Church (in the center of the illustration, and the oldest religious congregation in Galveston) and, clockwise from lower left: Eaton Chapel of Trinity Episcopal, Sacred Heart Catholic, Saint Mary's Cathedral, and Temple B'Nai Israel.

Historically, the congregations and clergy of the city have shared a cooperative, open relationship, working closely together for the good of the community. The title of this painting, "Hold On To Your Faith, But Respect the Faith of Others," is a quote from the teachings of Rabbi Henry Cohen, who served the Temple B'Nai Israel for fifty years. Rabbi Cohen was a very influential leader in the secular and religious community from 1885 until his death in 1952. This quote sums up the way in which he lived and served his community and the values he tried to instill in others.

America's grand experiment to suppress hard liquor in the 1920s provided Galveston with another opportunity. Rum-running cargo vessels from England, anchored in the Gulf beyond U.S. jurisdiction, were met by small, fast speedboats owned by Galveston gangs. The smugglers offloaded choice whiskey and brought it ashore on the beach, or at private docks, and sometimes at Rollover on the Bolivar Peninsula. Hiding the cases temporarily among the pilings behind the latticework of Galveston homes, the mobsters then shipped it by rail, truck, or automobile into the nation, even as far as Cleveland. The town experienced a struggle to rule among the mobsters, gangland killings with bodies dumped on the beach, and shootouts on the streets.

In the 1920s two remarkable brothers, Sam and Rosario Maceo, immigrants from Leesville, Louisiana with roots in Palermo, Sicily, brought order to the illegal liquor business. They combined it with illegal gambling and nightclubs. Their Balinese Room, located at the end of a 200-foot dock off the seawall, became one of the most famous night spots of the Gulf Coast. They provided dance bands, dinner, drinks, and gambling tables that folded into the wall. The brothers gave money to charities and churches, suppressed gang violence, sponsored civic events, and imported such celebrities as Phil Harris. They were well-liked in the community and Galveston extended the Maceos the same easy toleration given to the madams. Residents took pride in their adopted sobriquet, "The Free State of Galveston."

It all came to an end in the 1950s. The Internal Revenue Service launched investigations into the Maceo operation, and state officials brought injunctions to halt the gambling and prostitution. Texas Rangers confiscated slot machines, smashed them with sledgehammers, and dumped them into Galveston Bay. Sam Maceo died of cancer in 1951, his brother of heart disease in 1953. The brains of the system were gone. The gamblers and prostitutes left the island and "The Free State of Galveston" came to an end. What was left behind was the beach—which had always been an attraction—a declining port, a medical school, and block after block of decayed Victorian homes and buildings.

These were the foundation stones for the future, the basis for the second phase of Galveston's evolution into a tourist city.

The University of Texas Medical Branch (UTMB) continued to grow with the state's need for doctors. It had been awarded to the Island City by state referendum in 1881, because nowhere else in Texas was there such a variety of diseases for students to experience—indeed, a dubious distinction for the town. The school survived and grew, at least in part through the generosity of the Sealys, a prominent local merchant family. John Sealy gave the money to build the first hospital, created a foundation, and paid the annual school deficits. UTMB eventually embraced fifty buildings on eighty acres behind the seawall. It became the city's largest employer and aided the local economy, but as a state agency it paid no taxes.

The port struggled to maintain its position as a cotton export point, explored the opportunity for sulphur and grain shipments, but sank in comparison with the port of Houston, which became the second greatest port of the nation on a foundation of petroleum products. The blue-water vessels simply glided past the old harbor on their way through Galveston Bay to the Houston Ship Channel, which opened in 1914.

Galveston's salvation was to develop as a family-oriented recreation area for Houston and Texas. Earlier in the century, the chamber of commerce recognized the value in attracting conventions and in sponsoring city celebrations such as the Pageant of Pulchritude, a bathing-beauty contest of the 1920s. In the late 1950s, after the end of the vice trade, the city discovered the usefulness of its old buildings. Anne A. Brindley, who was active both in the chamber of commerce and in the Texas State Historical Association, rallied the elite to form the Galveston Historical Foundation in order to save the Williams-Tucker House, one of the oldest houses on the island. It opened to the public, and Galvestonians discovered that visitors were interested in such places. The historical organization, aided particularly by wealthy contributors such as the Moody Foundation and oilman George Mitchell, became instrumental in a series of restorations along

"Do Good For Good's Sake, Not For Hope of Reward" —Cohen

DO GOOD FOR GOOD'S SAKE, NOT FOR HOPE OF REWARD

The bungalow in the painting is called the Rabbinage, the home of the Rabbi of Congregation B'Nai Israel. However, the real subject of the piece is Rabbi Henry Cohen, the day he discovered a young girl sitting on the curb crying. He approached her to inquire into the nature of her distress. She told him that she was a Catholic ready to make her communion, but because her family was very poor, they could not afford to buy her a white dress for her confirmation and first communion. After comforting her he sent her on her way and went himself to Levy's Department Store (Mr. Levy was a member of his congregation), bought a white communion dress, and had it delivered to the child's home. The following Sunday, a very happy little girl took her first communion.

Among the many writings of Rabbi Cohen are his notes for the instruction of youth. The quote in the title of this painting, "Do Good for Good's Sake, Not For Hope of Reward," must have been frequently used, as it is underscored many times.

"OLD RED"—THE UNIVERSITY OF TEXAS MEDICAL BRANCH

In 1873 Dr. Ashbel Smith, who was at one time Surgeon General of the Republic of Texas, reorganized Galveston Medical College. It was then called the Texas Medical College, and it later became the Medical Branch of the University of Texas. The original building seen here was designed by Nicholas Clayton after he spent time visiting other medical facilities around the United States. The result of his research was a plan, that was approved, for a building in the Romanesque style. Unique to "Old Red" is the intricate brickwork done by Mr. Clayton's favorite master brick mason, Denny Devlin. In the 1900 hurricane, the towers were lost, as well as the spires on each of the six columns across the front of the building. "Old Red" remained unused for many years, and many other buildings crowded in around it. In 1984, however, it was carefully restored and is in use again today. Although the building carries the official name "Ashbel Smith," the students and faculty often refer to it by its nickname, "Old Red."

The official seal, ghosted through the painting, was replaced in 1970 by one which was similar to the seals representing the other branches of the university. With permission from the Board of Regents the artist chose to use this original seal, as it more uniquely symbolizes the medical profession and also it is a part of the history of "Old Red."

THE *ELISSA* AT THE FIVE-MILE JETTY LIGHTHOUSE

As this 105-year-old iron barque passed the five-mile jetty lighthouse in September of 1982, a new life began for her. She was launched in 1877 in Aberdeen, Scotland, and sailed under many national flags through the years. She visited Galveston in 1883 and again in 1886. But by 1975 she was rusted and badly leaking, and was about to be sold to the scrap yard in Piraeus, Greece, when she was purchased by the Galveston Historical Foundation, which set about restoring her and towing her back to Texas from Piraeus. Today, after several years of expensive restoration, she floats gracefully at Pier 21 in the historic strand district of Galveston, telling her story of life at sea during the Age of Sails. From time to time, manned by well-trained volunteers, she tests her readiness in sea trials, and in 1986 the *Elissa* sailed into New York harbor for the Statue of Liberty celebra-

tion. There, she proudly represented Texas in the International Parade of Tall Ships.

The lighthouse which stands at the end of the five-mile jetty, guiding ships through the entrance to the pass into Galveston Bay, is the most recent of the Galveston Bay lights. Originally planned as a wooden structure, it was changed to metal as a result of the 1900 hurricane nearly wiping out Galveston. As exposed as it was, however, succeeding hurricanes also took their toll on it. Finally, in 1916, after much reinforcing, the lighthouse was manned and lighted, only to be extinguished during the years of World War I. It was again lighted when the U.S. Navy lifted the blackout in November 1918. Today, automatically illuminated, the lighthouse still serves its purpose, but the only residents still there are the gulls and pelicans.

Broadway and the old business area of the Strand. The most sensational piece of historic restoration, however, was that of the tall ship *Elissa*.

The foundation recovered the iron hull of the ship from a shipyard in Piraeus, Greece. Craftsmen and volunteer workers from around the country worked to restore the square-rigged vessel and in 1982, after an investment of $3.6 million, the "tall ship for Texas" sailed once more. Its permanent berth was in Galveston, but the *Elissa* joined the parade of sailing vessels sent to New York to commemorate the restoration of the Statue of Liberty. It still goes on annual cruises, sailed by the volunteers who maintain it. For the most part, the *Elissa* brings attention to Galveston and serves as a tourist attraction.

The city acquired other facilities for visitors, such as Moody Gardens, which enclosed a rain-forest garden under a glass pyramid. There were also new city celebrations, such as "Dickens on the Strand," a tightly controlled spring-break celebration for students, Mardi Gras, and an annual sand-castle-building contest on the beach. Through all of this effort to bring guests to the city, it was the beach, according to various polls of visitors, that remained the chief reason for traveling to Galveston. Without the beach, the town would be much less attractive. Acting upon that knowledge, the city council in late 1994 authorized spending $5.9 million for a beach-restoration project in front of the seawall.

It is a natural phenomenon that the sea will move up to a seawall and wash away the sand. This happened to the seawall in Galveston except where the wall slanted inward at Stewart Beach and on the lee side of the south jetty, where sand actually accumulated. Earlier attempts to preserve the sand with rock groins thrusting like fingers from the seawall more or less failed. The groins proved useful for fishing, but were a hazard for swimmers. The beach by and large disappeared, and so to preserve tourism the city moved to restore it. The task was accomplished with large pipes and a suction pump excavating off-beach sand in the Gulf and depositing it to the front of the seawall. Other coastal beaches have been thus restored, but it remains to be

seen how long it will last at Galveston. The natural tendency is for the beach to erode again in front of the seawall, and therefore continual beach renourishment has been planned. To underscore the conversion to a family-oriented resort, moreover, the Galveston City Council banned the use of liquor on its beaches.

The beach "down the island," a local expression for that part of the island beyond the seawall, has migrated landward, and the off-ramp at the end of the seawall which led to the western beaches as late as 1965 now ends in water. The island has shifted, and Hurricane Alicia in 1983 helped push it along. The Open Beaches Act of 1959 designated Texas beaches as public property from the surf back to the vegetation line of the dunes. The law was intended to preserve the shore for all the people, not just for the rich who could afford to buy the land and fence it. Without asking, Hurricane Alicia shifted the shoreline and residents found their stilted homes standing on public land. It brought the traditions of private property into a clash with public interest. The result was that such owners were permitted to continue to utilize serviceable homes, but not to rebuild.

Far beyond the seawall that protects the main city, there are now communities of expensive vacation houses and condominiums on sand barely a few feet above sea level. Some are located on such a narrowing strip of land that both bay and Gulf waters, less than a mile apart, can be seen from the central roadway. The beach is eroding at a rate of one to two feet per year. It is not difficult to foresee that destruction surely will come to this part of the sand-barrier island.

The history of Galveston Island, nevertheless, is heroic, tragic, and fascinating. Lured originally by its natural harbor, but sustained by the primordial call of the beach that beckons all human beings, people have chosen to make a home on this island. It has a hostile environment—both subtle, with its corrosive salt-laden sea breezes, and obvious, with its periodic roaring hurricanes. Still, this island, with its oleanders, palm trees, pastel sunsets, exotic stilted houses, warm sunshine, and daily gifts of seashells from the Gulf, possesses a charm that residents and visitors cannot resist. It is indeed a different place.

THE STRAND OF GALVESTON

As a result of her vulnerability to the elements (hurricanes), the discontinuation of gambling, and the decline of industry at the port, Galveston suffered economic decline. Something had to be done—and it was! In the 1960s, a two-year study pointed out Galveston's historical significance and the possibility of attracting the tourist trade. Such places as the Strand, Ashton Villa, Old Red, and the George Sealy house were purchased with funds provided by such interested patrons as the Moody Foundation and the Kempner Fund. As a result, the Historical Foundation was able to take over six Strand buildings with the idea of selling them to those who would covenant to restore the buildings without altering their outer appearance. This was the beginning of the restoration of the area of Galveston known as the Strand. Today, the buildings are restored to their original beauty and within them one may dine on sumptuous meals, browse in shops and boutiques, and even stay the night in the magnificent Tremont Hotel.

In December the Strand comes alive with "Dickens on the Strand," and in late winter Mardi Gras is celebrated, having been revived after it was discontinued during World War II.

The historic preservation movement of Galveston has also resulted in the creation of the East End Historic District and the Silk Stocking Historic Precinct. The Grand Opera House, the Railroad Museum, and the 1861 Custom House all lure tourists to one of the most historic cities in Texas.

THE BEACH HOTEL

If it still existed, the Beach Hotel would today be standing in water below Seawall Boulevard and 23rd Street, not far from the present-day Galvez Hotel. It was opened in 1883 as Galveston's first real attraction for vacationers. It was architect Nicholas Clayton's favorite building design, one which he felt was his crowning achievement. The carpentry of this building, like that of the Electric Pavilion, has never been duplicated. In 1898 this beautiful, entirely wooden three-story structure, so gloriously painted in mauve and electric green, with a red-and-white striped roof, caught fire and was totally destroyed as Mr. Clayton, sick in his bed, watched from his window.

Nicholas Clayton died in 1916, and many years later his widow, Mary Lorena, expressed to a close family friend—Rabbi Henry Cohen, the beloved Rabbi of Temple B'Nai Israel—her desire for a suitable monument dedicated to the memory of her husband. The rabbi replied softly, "Oh, you don't need one, my dear, he's got them all over town. Just go around and read some of the cornerstones."

"PROTECTORS OF THE COAST"
NAVY BLIMP BASE - HITCHCOCK, TEXAS
1943

PROTECTORS OF THE COAST: NAVY BLIMP BASE—HITCHCOCK, 1943

In 1942 it was known that German U-boats called "Wolf Packs" were inflicting heavy damage on trans-ocean American shipping and were patrolling the darkened shore of the southern Gulf coast, taking reconnaissance of rich sources of petroleum and gasoline. To protect the military installations and these vital industries, a blimp base was built at Hitchcock, Texas, fifteen miles north of Galveston. It was commissioned in 1943, where the navy built one of the largest wooden buildings in the world, capable of housing up to six "K Class" blimps at one time. It was 1,000 feet long, 300 feet wide, over 200 feet high, and covered 300,000 square feet of floor space. Outside was a stabilized blacktop circular mat covering nearly eighty acres. The Hitchcock base was the second of its kind to protect the Gulf coast, the first being located at Houma, Louisiana. The blimps from these two bases patrolled the area, searching out and finding a number of submarines and radioing in for the patrol boats to make the kill. These nearly silent blimps had the ability to slow down and hover over possible targets to give an accurate reading of their location. It was partly on account of them that no damage was ever inflicted on the coast by the enemy.

After the war, the base and its huge hangar were used for storage, and during the Korean conflict they were used as a repair depot for tanks and other heavy equipment. Eventually the property was sold into private ownership and the huge hangar was dismantled. Today, all that remains of that enormous structure are four concrete pillars so large they can be seen from Galveston, looking north across Galveston Bay.

PELICANS AND SHRIMP BOATS

To observe the pelicans that abundantly inhabit the entire coastline, one need only to find the harbors where the shrimp boats are docked. There, the birds find calm waters and plenty of food to their liking.

The largest populations of both brown and white pelicans are found in their nesting grounds around Galveston and Matagorda Bay and on Pelican Island in Corpus Christi Bay.

Today the brown pelicans number more than 5,000, but they weren't always so numerous. In the 1950s they quit nesting, and by 1966 only 20 brown pelicans were counted in the census. The cause was suspected to be a pesticide which may have come from the Mississippi River or perhaps from mosquito spraying along the coast. After years of research and constant protection by the Texas Parks and Wildlife Department, it is possible once again to enjoy the beauty of these birds floating gracefully in the water, soaring above, and playfully diving for their dinner.

As I watched these magnificent birds with their fat bodies, oversized wings, and such large bills, wondering how they are able to fly with their catch, I remembered a poem from my childhood which began:

What a wonderful bird is the pelican
His bill can hold more than his belly can. . . .

Truly they are wonderful creatures and we must take care to see that they always remain with us by keeping the ecology of our fragile coastline in balance.

THE BRAZOS LANDING

The roadway down Galveston Island leads to a tollbridge at San Luis Pass, the shallow stretch of water that separates Galveston from Follets Island. Although called an island, it is really a sandy peninsula affixed to the mainland near the mouth of the fabled Brazos River. In the late 1830s Robert Mills, a rich Brazoria merchant and planter, along with others, tried to establish a port on a small island at this pass. Storms, however, filled the potential harbor with sand by 1842 and San Luis Island eventually attached itself to the peninsula that stretched from the mainland. The pass remained shallow, and in the early 1900s a man wading across it was reported to have been killed in a rare shark attack.

Several small, exposed vacation communities such as Surfside now face the Gulf and continue a resort tradition that reaches back to the nineteenth century. Surfside, or Surfside Beach as it is sometimes called, was once a part of Velasco, a port town on the east bank of the Brazos River where it flowed into the Gulf of Mexico. The schooner *Lively* landed thirty-eight men at this point in 1821 to begin Stephen F. Austin's colonization of Texas, and ten years later Mexico established a customs checkpoint at the site. In the early 1830s Mary Austin Holley visited Velasco and described it in her book, *Texas:*

Velasco is the resort, in summer, of great numbers of visiters [sic] from the north of the colony, who come to enjoy the delightful seabreezes, sea bathing, and the comforts with which they are every where surrounded. Excellent accommodations can always be obtained at boarding houses, which, among other attractions, are always furnished with supplies of oysters and fish of the first quality. Musqutoe [sic] bars are not often needed here, and, altogether, it is one of the most delightful places in the country.[1]

Across the mouth of the river, on the west bank, the merchant firm of McKinney, Williams and Company established the rival town of Quintana in the 1830s. Samuel May Williams was a Galveston businessman and Thomas F. McKinney was a former keelboat man and supply agent for Texas revolutionaries.

McKinney, reputedly, cleaned his teeth with a Bowie knife, wore a scarlet frock coat made from a blanket, and once paddled down the Brazos River in a hog trough made from a hollowed-out log. Along the Quintana beach, wealthy plantation owners built family vacation homes to escape the summer heat of Texas. Both places served as gateways of immigration and as supply points for settlers moving up the Brazos Valley into the Austin Colony. River ports such as Brazoria, San Felipe de Austin, Richmond, and Washington-on-the-Brazos sprang up as interior shipping points for cotton and as focal points of activity.

In 1832, during the unrest preceding the Texas Revolution, Henry Smith and John Austin—who was perhaps distantly related to Stephen F. Austin—tried to transport artillery from Brazoria down the river and around the coast to Anahuac on Trinity Bay. The cannons were to be used to uproot a troublesome Mexican garrison. Juan Davis Bradburn, under instructions from his government, had established a Mexican customs house at Anahuac, high in Galveston Bay, and had ordered all imports to clear through his port. It was a nuisance to shipowners. This and the arrest of William Barret Travis brought armed resistance against Bradburn. John Austin helped lead the protest. At Brazoria, a town John Austin founded, he took two small cannons left behind by the steamboat *Ariel* in 1830, transferred them with men to the schooner *Brazoria*, and sailed downstream. At Velasco the Mexican garrison under Colonel Don Domingo de Ugartechea stood at arms to block his passage.

In the ensuing fight the rebels, protected by cotton bales on the schooner, banged away with their small cannons, while Texan sharpshooters on land prevented the Mexican gunners from manning their own artillery. Estimates of the number of men involved vary between 100 and 200 per side, but after both sides had suffered similar casualties of about 21 men, the Mexicans ran out of ammunition and surrendered. The prisoners were allowed to return to Mexico and, meanwhile, the trouble at Anahuac was settled peaceably. John Austin died several months later of cholera. Despite its peaceful resolution, the fight revealed the temper of the times, and the Battle of Velasco was looked

HIGH AND DRY

After World War I, commercial shrimping in the area evolved from a small part-time industry to the most valuable sea fishery in the United States. Texas fishermen played a major part in its development. In early times, cast nets and seines were used, but later on boats were designed to drag trawls (cone-shaped nets with two wings on each side) along the floor of the bay and as a result, seines became obsolete. Modern shrimp boats come in several sizes. The smallest are called "mosquito" boats and they usually do their shrimping in the bay area with only one trawl net. Others are large ocean vessels called super trawlers that venture far into the Gulf and are double-rigged (having two trawls which can be pulled simultaneously). These large vessels are equipped with up-to-date navigational aids, including radar, ship-to-shore radios, and fish finders.

Today, because of the threat to the endangered sea turtles, the trawls must be equipped with turtle-excluder devices when fishing in federal or state waters, and the U.S. Coast Guard is diligent in monitoring the vessels to see that they comply.

upon as the first bloodshed of the Texas Revolution that boiled over several years later.[2]

At the end of the revolution in 1836, President David G. Burnet declared Velasco a temporary capital for the Republic of Texas and signed the peace treaties there with defeated General Antonio Lopez de Santa Anna. Both sides failed to carry out the agreements fully, but Mexican troops withdrew and Texas became independent. The twin towns at the mouth of the Brazos again took up the activities of commerce, migration, and recreation as the Brazos Valley prospered, as part of the cotton kingdom of the American South. During the Civil War the towns were fortified and served as embarkation points for blockade runners. Union ships replied with bombardment and the towns declined as resort areas: No one cared to get shot at with cannons. This decline continued during the impoverished Reconstruction era after the war.

There were, moreover, two overwhelming obstacles to urban success, caused by natural circumstances. One of them was the Brazos River. It was the longest and largest stream in Texas, and ran generally southeastward from the high plains to the Gulf of Mexico. When flowing through the flat coastal plain, the stream seemingly lost its sense of purpose and became sluggish, brown with mud, and meandering. It flooded at times, constantly dumped its heavy load of silt where it met the placid salt water of the gulf, and created a difficult sandbar on top of a layer of blue clay.[3] Mary Austin Holley described the bar as twenty feet wide with a six-foot depth of water over it. The bar was a "serious obstruction," she said, and in addition, progress was slow on the winding river. Traveling to Texas Holley took six days to reach her destination—three days from New Orleans to the mouth of the Brazos and three days from the mouth to Brazoria, thirty miles upstream. It was faster for passengers to get off and walk once they reached the mainland.[4]

An attempt in 1854 to circumvent the bar at Velasco with a canal into the shallow West Bay that led to Galveston was only a partial success. The canal failed to profit and, moreover, faced competition from a new transportation technology.[5] Because of obstructions and delays on the river, Brazos Valley planters opted to haul their cotton overland on muddy roads with slow ox-teams to Houston.[6] It was to be expected, then, that entrepreneurs would build the first railroad in Texas, the Buffalo Bayou, Brazos, and Colorado, in 1852 to connect the valley planters with the transportation corridor established between Galveston and Houston.[7] The sandbar at the Brazos mouth and the desultory nature of the river were thus minimized, but they continued to cause some difficulty in the twentieth century.

The other major problem for the area involved the Gulf hurricanes that periodically attacked the Texas coast. In 1875, in 1886, and again in 1900 hurricanes hammered the Brazos area. In 1875 the town of Velasco was so inundated that it lost its town records, and after the 1886 storm the residents decided to desert the beach and move four miles inland. New Velasco was established in 1891. Despite the move, the 1900 storm wrecked the new town and left Velasco groggy for decades. Quintana suffered the same fate; the 1900 hurricane scoured clean the coastline of Brazoria County. Most of the people of Quintana abandoned the shore to the seagulls and tourists, and moved inland for safety. Stubborn Albert Coveney, who had lost his home, stayed, and rebuilt with walls four layers thick. He was familiar with ship construction, so he put his home together so that it might float away, but never blow away. The house stands today as a historic site integrated into Quintana Beach County Park. The situation at the mouth of the Brazos, however, resulted in the same sort of grudging respect for hurricanes that had been forced upon the residents of the Bolivar Peninsula.

This early history of the lower Brazos River is obscure today and only a few old houses, such as Coveney's, bear silent witness to the events of that time. The lights and flares from fantasy-like refineries scattered upon the green coastal plain, together with the new towns of the petrochemical industry, now define the coastal countryside. Freeport, located three miles above the mouth of the difficult Brazos, began in 1912 as a port "free" of dockage fees, to exploit the sulphur mined from the nearby Bryan Mound. Using the Frasch method of forcing hot water into the ground to dissolve the sulphur and then pumping it out again, engineers exhausted the dome by 1935. Later, in the 1970s, following the scare over fuel shortages, the vast, empty underground caverns of the mound were pumped full of crude oil to serve as a national reserve.

Freeport, meanwhile, tried to solve the old harbor problem. Jetties had been built in 1880, and were rebuilt in 1888 with the hope of funneling the slow current so that it would scour a channel through the sandbar. Hurricanes, however, choked the mouth with sand. In 1919 the U.S. government completed a dredging operation that provided a depth of twenty feet. Within six days, even before the dredge boat had a chance to leave, the channel measured only fifteen feet deep as the river continued its age-old silting process. In 1921 a sulphur ship entered in eighteen-and-a-half feet of water, only to have the river drop a load of sand and maroon the vessel even before it could be loaded.

Finally, the Brazos River Harbor Navigation District formed in 1925 to resolve the problem. The engineers cut a diversion channel for the river to carry off the silt, built a bridge over the new course before the water was released, and after that dredged the original mouth and stream bed into a deep-water harbor. The new port was completed in 1954. Meanwhile, in 1929, the Texas legislature established the Brazos River Authority, which represented the first attempt in the United States to manage the water resources of an entire river basin. This affected sixty-five counties and eventually resulted in the construction of a series of dams and reservoirs.[8] John Graves memorialized this change in the upper Brazos with his nostalgic book *Goodbye to a River*, published in 1961. The upper part of the river and its history would never be the same; the same was true for the lower portion as well.

After five million tons of sulphur had been extracted and the resource depleted, Freeport dwindled to the level of a sluggish fishing village. Dow Chemical Company, however, arrived in 1939. The company was initially interested in extracting magnesium from sea water, but then became involved with constructing petrochemical facilities that could utilize Texas' raw materials of salt, oil, gas, sulphur, and water. This was a part of the develop-

ment of the vast petrochemical complex of coastal Texas that eventually reached from Freeport to Port Arthur. Dow's timing was perfect: World War II struck, and the federal government needed petrochemical products such as artificial rubber and aviation fuel. Contracts, population, and money poured into the region, Dow Chemical Company profited, and the lower Brazos Valley was transformed.

Dow arrived in 1940 with 14,000 workers. The appalled city leaders at Velasco refused to accept expansion even though the company offered to build homes and pay the costs. The result was that seven miles away, Dow built the new town of Lake Jackson, named for the plantation owner who once owned the land. Alden Dow, son of the founder of the chemical company, laid out the city and called the main roads "drives" and the streets to the business district "ways." This provided the opportunity to whimsically name certain streets "This Way," "That Way," "Any Way," and "His Way" (the last being the road in front of a church, not a street honoring Frank Sinatra). The company donated the streets, parks, water and sewer systems, and fire equipment. It was not intended as a company town, though, and people bought their own homes. The land, however, was humid, hot, and boggy. Mosquitoes blackened the screendoors. As workers struggled with the forests and drainage, the following anonymous ditty circulated:

So this, my dear, is Lake Jackson,
The town that was built in a swamp,
Where the streets wind like snakes in a huddle,
And the people will live without pomp.[9]

Lake Jackson incorporated in 1944 and continued to grow with the expansion of Dow Chemical Company, now covering 5,000 acres, and the other companies that came to link into the petrochemical maze. One company's output became another's input. During World War II the name "Brazosport" came into general use as an inclusive term for the towns of Freeport, Lake Jackson, Quintana, Surfside, and the other small towns near the mouth of the Brazos. In 1944 the mayors established a joint Chamber of Commerce and residents formed a Brazosport Independent School District. Every July they celebrate the Great Texas Mosquito Festival together. This is the urban enactment of the adage "When life serves you lemons, make lemonade."

In 1957, when Velasco merged with Freeport, the past joined the present. Still, it seems as if this land has had two histories—that of early Texas, with colonization and revolution, and that of twentieth-century Texas, with science and technology. For the visitor today, the distant past is hardly visible, and there is little connection to the present. Surrounding the old site of Quintana, for example, are the tanks and silver towers of the petrochemical industry. Pilgrims must look upstream to Washington-on-the-Brazos or to West Columbia to find museums that portray revolutionary history and antebellum life. There seem to be in this immediate coastal area but few artists, singers, poets, architects, or writers to link the old and the new Texas—there is no John Graves of the lower Brazos.

At Lake Jackson and Clute there exist a museum of natural science and a Sea Center concerned with marine fisheries. Their presence reflects the science and technology interests of the neighborhood. Although there has been some planning for a general historical museum in Lake Jackson, it is not yet open. The employees in the petrochemical plants are migrants focused upon their work. They are not bad people, just rootless, with little connection to the lower Brazos.[10] They will not linger beyond the time when the resources are gone; there is no expressed love of the land; the past has been brushed aside. Perhaps that has always been true of Americans seeking opportunity. Yet it was here, in this verdant coastal land, that Texas was born and in which it found early nourishment.

TROUBLED WATERS

AT MATAGORDA BAY

Elsewhere on the Texas coast—Port Arthur, Galveston, Brazosport, Corpus Christi—the ingenuity of technology and the seduction of profit obscure the imperative of the sea. Along this central part of the Texas coast, however, the struggle between human ambition and natural physics is conspicuous. If you look at a travel map of the state, such as that issued by the Texas Department of Transportation, for example, it is easy to see the route of the Gulf Intracoastal Waterway—dashed lines through the bays and a blue slash through the mainland. The exaggeration on the map actually makes Follets Island and Surfside Beach appear detached from the coast. They really are not. The roadways do not follow the route of the Intracoastal Waterway and so from the highway this technical triumph is easy to miss.

The waterway, a barge canal measuring 125 feet wide and 12 feet deep, runs from Brownsville to Fort Myers, Florida, and accounts for about 70 percent of the barge traffic of the Gulf Coast. Petroleum, coal, and other minerals are the main items transported. Portions of the canal system were built earlier, some as far back as the nineteenth century, but it was completed in 1949. The Gulf Intracoastal Waterway links together the deep-water ports of the state like the cord holding together a string of pearls. The canal is technically successful, enormously profitable, and quietly controversial. Nature will not surrender to this manmade alteration along the shoreline. The U.S. Army Corps of Engineers continually dredges to keep up with shoaling and dumps the muck alongside the canal in spoil banks and "islands."[1] It is a never-ending war.

The waterway's struggle with nature is manifest at Sargent Beach, which is close to East Matagorda Bay and southwest of Brazosport. Named for George Sargent from Cornwall, England, who settled in the coastal country to raise cattle and cotton in the mid-nineteenth century, the sandy beach on the coast was reputedly one of the best in Texas in the 1940s.[2] A vacation community developed of some six to ten streets of stilted cottages, but since then the beach has so eroded that only one row re-

mains. No one is certain why the Gulf gobbled twenty-five to thirty-six feet of shore per year—it may be because of hurricanes, tidal changes, a rise in sea-level, dams on the Brazos River, or the interruption of sand-carrying currents by port construction at Brazosport; whatever the reason, the result was the loss of the shore.[3] There was not enough tourist demand to consider nourishment of the beach, and the cottages fell one by one into the hungry surf.

The Intracoastal Waterway, which cuts behind the beach on the mainland, is now threatened by the relentless Gulf waters, only one-quarter mile away. If breached, the canal would close at this point, since the shallow-draft barges are not designed to operate in open sea conditions. At the moment, with completion planned for 1998, the Corps of Engineers is building an eight-mile revetment of granite blocks sunk into the remaining sand as an underground seawall. In three to five years, it is expected that the sea will reach the wall and stop. Sargent Beach is already gone, but perhaps the waterway will be spared.[4] The struggle between engineers and mother nature is apparent and ongoing here. The Corps is betting $80 million that it will win the contest.

The barge canal continues southwestward along the mainland and then across Matagorda Bay, behind the protection of the Matagorda peninsula. It follows the curve of the coastline to Brownsville, provides cheap transportation, disrupts wildlife, and raises the blood pressure of environmental groups. In Matagorda Bay, however, the barges and spoil banks merely disturb the bay shrimpers sailing out of Palacios and Port Lavaca. There is not so much activity here, compared with Galveston or Corpus Christi bays. The shallow inlet, with its various small rivers and estuaries, nonetheless, is one of the large bays along the Texas coastline. Its shape was influenced by the Colorado River, which released so much sediment after the removal of a legendary log jam in the 1920s that a delta reached across to Matagorda peninsula and created East Matagorda Bay. Eventually, the town of Matagorda, once a seaport, became landlocked and the river became useless for transportation.

Historically, however, Matagorda Bay played an interesting role in the life of Texas. The Spanish, starting in 1519 with Alonso Alvarez de Piñeda, a navy lieutenant, explored the Gulf Coast. Cartographers followed, and in 1691 Manuel Joseph de Cardenas, an engineer, drew a detailed map of the bay. The Spanish had been searching for Fort St. Louis, which had been established by the French explorer, René Robert Cavelier, Sieur de La Salle, in 1685 at Garcitas Creek in the upper bay region. La Salle, who had explored the Mississippi River, had returned with 280 settlers to establish French control of that great river. He overshot the mark and landed at Matagorda Bay. It may be that he thought he was in the confused delta region of the Mississippi. His colony shortly foundered: The settlers died of disease, overwork, and Indian hostility. La Salle, moody and stubborn, was murdered—shot in the head—by his own men.[5]

The Spanish, not knowing that La Salle's colony had failed, meanwhile sent out eleven different expeditions to locate and root out these intrusive French people from land they considered part of the Spanish domain. Only ruins and five children, captives of the Karankawa Indians, remained in 1689 when Alonso de León finally found the fort and asserted Spanish sovereignty. Supposedly, it was at this same site that Marqués de Aguayo, the provincial governor, built the Presidio La Bahía in 1721. The following year, he authorized the construction of the Mission La Bahía on the other side of the creek. In 1726 the Spanish settlers, prompted by mosquitoes and Indians, moved the presidio and mission inland, thus abandoning the unhappy coastal area.

Recently, an echo from this early history has been heard, in the form of one of the original French ships. La Salle had originally sailed from France with four ships. Spanish privateers captured one ship en route; an escort vessel returned home; the supply ship sank at the entrance to the bay; and La Salle used his last vessel for transporting materials from his grounded supply ship to his fort. This last one, the bark Belle, a personal gift from the French King Louis XIV, went aground on the Matagorda Peninsula in 1686 after being driven across the bay by a norther. Its fifty-one-foot hull settled into the mud twelve feet underwater, and remained as a snag for shrimper's nets 300 years later.

In 1978, Barto Arnold III, a marine archaeologist working for the Texas Historical Commission, began a search for the wreck of the Belle. He located the wreck site by measuring magnetic differences in the area. In 1995 groping divers brought up an ornate 800-pound bronze cannon that verified the Belle. The archaeologists constructed a cofferdam, pumped out the murky water, and excavated a site on the open bay floor. This was a unique effort and they found pots, lead shot, glass trading beads, a complete skeleton (nicknamed "Dead Bob" by lab workers), coils of rope, plates, and barrels. It was one of the more spectacular excavations of a shipwreck along the Texas coast. Dead Bob's skull revealed that he suffered from tooth decay, a broken nose and cheekbone, and a concussion that left a four-inch crack in the bone.[6] Life was not easy in the seventeenth century.

Arnold's magnetometer, with its ability to detect iron, revealed at least 200 other sunken ships in Matagorda Bay. They are of more recent vintage than the Belle, but the numbers indicate the degree of activity of past shipping in the bay. It is in contrast to the generally small-scale bay shrimping business that predominates today. In the nineteenth century Matagorda Bay promised to surpass Galveston as the Texas gateway for commerce and immigration. That promise, however, was washed away in the troubled waters of two severe, almost back-to-back hurricanes.

Before the storms, however, Carl, Prince of Solms Braunfels from Germany, identified Indian Point on the western bank as the best deep-water harbor within Matagorda Bay. Here, in 1844, he landed the first shipload of German immigrants on their way to lands in the hilly country north and east of San Antonio. Mary A. Maverick, then living at DeCrow's Point at the opening of the bay, noted in her memoirs:

Half Moon Reef Lighthouse - 1888

HALFMOON REEF LIGHTHOUSE

In 1858 a light was established by the Lighthouse Board on the southern extremity of Halfmoon Reef in Matagorda Bay. It was hexagonal in shape, consisting of three small rooms. Its outer walls were painted white for a day mark and it had a round domed light in the center of the roof for a night mark. Its purpose was to steer ships away from the shallow waters and guide them through the bay to safe harbor at Indianola.

In 1861 the Confederates extinguished the light but inflicted little damage on the lighthouse, and it was relighted at the end of the Civil War. It is known to have been occupied for some years by a keeper, his wife, and their six children. Supplies were brought to them in a skiff once every three months.

The light remained active until 1885 and then became a day mark only, until it was removed by the U.S. Coast Guard. Today, it graces a small park near the bridge in Port Lavaca and is lovingly cared for by the Calhoun County Historical Society.

LASALLE AND THE KARANKAWAS—MATAGORDA BAY, 1686

René Robert Cavelier Sieur De LaSalle was seeking the mouth of the Mississippi River, but because of faulty maps and miscalculations, he landed instead on the Texas coast in what is now Matagorda Bay. His ill-fated voyage was further complicated by the appearance of a tall, dark, well-proportioned native of the Karankawa nation. The tattooed man was completely naked except for a few pieces of cloth he found washed ashore and braided into his long hair. The rattle from a rattlesnake finished the braid and his body was covered with dark, smelly alligator grease he used for warding off mosquitoes. He was friendly at first, but lack of communication and strange customs eventually made them enemies. Both of LaSalle's ships—the *Belle*, in which he sailed, and the *Amiable*—were lost, and sometime later when he began his overland journey to find civilization, LaSalle was killed, as were most of his men. But LaSalle and his adventures have recently come alive once again with the discovery in 1995 in Matagorda Bay of his two ships. The treasure of artifacts found within the hull of the *Belle* may reveal even more of this important time in Texas' colorful history.

General Somerville [Alexander Somerville, the customs agent] was a noted laugher—he saw the Prince's two attendants dress his Highness, that is lift him into his pants, and General Somerville was so overcome by the sight that he broke out into one of his famous fits of laughter, and was heard all over the point. The Prince and suite were all very courteous and polite to us. They wore cock feathers in their hats, and did not appear quite fitted to frontier life.[7]

Indian Point was actually a low island of crushed shell separated from the flat mainland by small brackish lakes. But the location lay west of the Trinity, Brazos, and Colorado Rivers—rivers that would not therefore have to be forded by immigrants—and oceangoing ships could come close enough to land people with the use of lighters. It was not ideal, but it was suitable. Indian Point developed into a port and changed its name to Indianola in 1849. It became an army depot during the war with Mexico and continued as a supply point for western forts over the next thirty years. Immigrants continued to pour through this place and it became the county seat. Indianola established a road to San Antonio, a turtle meat cannery, and transit facilities for the produce of the countryside. During the Civil War, in 1862, Union forces looted the town, and then occupied it in 1863 and 1864. After the war, as Texas recovered, the cattle empire surged and the world's first shipment of refrigerated beef moved on a Morgan steamer from Indianola to New Orleans. In 1875, with a population near 5,000, the port was thriving and its promise was bright. Then disaster struck.

With little warning from the fledgling U.S. Signal Service, the early national weather service, a hurricane hit dead center on Matagorda Bay on September 15–16, 1875. The inflowing tide flooded the streets chest-high and turned them into coursing rivers, undercut the new train tracks, smashed the docks to splinters caused a schooner, drifting backward, to destroy the telegraph office, and inundated the surrounding prairie land. There was no escape. Then, as the eye of the hurricane passed, the wind direction shifted to the northwest, and all of the water from the fifteen-foot storm surge that had been pushed twenty

miles inland now drained seaward, rushing out through the bay. The worst damage occurred with this flushing motion. Buildings with foundations that had been undermined first from the direction of the sea and then from the direction of the land collapsed, and some 300 people died. The storm cut twelve new bayous through the town site and left bodies strewn along the bay shore. Indianola, with three-fourths of its buildings gone, was left in a state of ruin.[8]

The damage to the entire bay area was extensive. The high sand dunes on Matagorda Island were washed flat and two bay lighthouses destroyed, though a large metal lighthouse which had recently been moved two miles onto higher ground survived. Ninety percent of the population of the small port of Saluria on the eastern tip of Matagorda Island were drowned. DeCrow's Point across the channel on the western tip of the peninsula was scoured of its cluster of buildings. A special storm-proof home built by Thomas DeCrow, a prominent rancher, had been uprooted and twenty-two people killed. DeCrow had sunk the corner posts six feet into the ground and connected cross braces. Only the shell of a cistern and a concrete outhouse remained. Nine months later Bishop R. W. B. Elliott, addressing a convention of the Protestant Episcopal Church, commented, "On Monday, January 24, accompanied by the Rev. Mr. Carrington and Mr. James McCoppin, lay reader, [I] went down in a wagon to La Salle [six miles south of Indianola] and took from the beach, where they had been cast up by the sea, the prayer desk, reading desk, lectern and altar of what was Ascension Church, Indianola."[9]

Saluria never recovered, but Indianola tried. The townspeople wanted to move the port to a higher elevation at Powder Horn Lake, three-and-a-half miles up a bayou. However, the Morgan Line, the most important shipping company on the coast, refused to help, and so Indianola remained at its vulnerable location. Some citizens moved permanently to other places; some merchants rebuilt; and other businessmen wisely opened branch stores at inland locations such as Victoria and San Antonio. The state and local counties offered tax relief for

1876 and the United States Life Saving Service placed a lifeboat station at the damaged site of Saluria. The county commissioners rebuilt the courthouse and the Signal Office began to experiment with storm-warning flags.

Again, however, in 1886, a strong hurricane struck with inadequate warning. By the time the Signal officer received information about the Gulf storm, the tide at Indianola was already on the rise. People were trapped in the same situation, only this time there were not so many people at the doomed port. The wind velocity was higher than before and the storm moved through faster. Thus, there was not as much flooding, but the railroad bed washed away and a fire broke out during the storm that destroyed much of the business district. A kerosene lamp exploded when the telegraphic office disintegrated and other wooden buildings caught fire in the midst of wind and rain.

This time there was even less reason to stay and rebuild. Transcontinental rail construction and Morgan Line intransigence preordained a gloomy economic future. In 1887, consequently, the county commissioners moved the seat of government to Lavaca, the local railroad abandoned the track, and the post office discontinued service. Movers stripped the old courthouse of everything useful—doors, windows, even the roof—and a fire destroyed the remaining business buildings. Indianola became a tragic ghost town with a story that offered a watery warning to those who would listen to the voice of the deep. The sea had won. Nearby Galvestonians who thought that they were somehow safe paid the price for their arrogance in 1900.

Matagorda Bay thus lost its economic promise with these storms of the nineteenth century, and its troubled, shallow waters offered possibilities only for shrimp fishing and small-scale recreation. It was just as well. Hurricane Carla in 1961 sent a tidal surge ten miles inland, reduced Port O'Connor at the tip of the mainland to "a pile of sand," as one resident described it, and damaged every building in the small resort town of Palacios at the head of the bay.[10] The inherent danger of the area seemingly forestalled petrochemical or other such economic activity. The bay's forced quiescence, however, may have served a useful purpose. It has remained quiet and unpolluted and thus contributed to one of the most remarkable conservation endeavors of the United States. This took place in the neighboring, smaller bays to the southwest.

INDIANOLA

Indianola was a seaport of major importance to both civilians and the military for over forty years. It was the closest seaport to the city of San Antonio, more than one hundred miles inland. By 1848, over 6,000 Germans had disembarked through this port and journeyed to found, among other places, the towns of New Braunfels and Fredericksburg. In addition, Italians, Moravians (Czechs), Alsatians, Irish, and people of many other nationalities set foot for the first time on U.S. soil at Indianola. Many continued inland, but many others stayed and plied their trade, making Indianola important enough to become the seat of government for Calhoun County from 1852 until 1886.

The U.S. Army's supplies were delivered here and soldiers disembarked here to make their way overland to the army's twenty-two forts on the western frontier. In 1859 Jefferson Davis, then U.S. secretary of war, experimented with importing camels from the Middle East to Indianola for the army to use as pack animals to cross the western desert. The experiment might have been successful but for the outbreak of the Civil War. The Union Army occupied Indianola in 1863. They tried to take Port Lavaca, eight miles to the north, but the local militia there fired its cannons from the town on the bluff and the two Union gunboats gave up and left.

By 1875 Indianola was a thriving city of between 3,000 and 3,500 people and an army depot of about 250 soldiers. This was the year of the first devastating hurricane, which killed 300 people and flooded and blew away most of the structures of the town. The second hurricane in 1886 not only wiped away the rest of the town, it filled in the bay with enough silt to render the port too shallow for ships, and the once-thriving town of Indianola passed into history.

MATAGORDA LIGHTHOUSE
C 1950

(PRECEDING PAGE)

MATAGORDA ISLAND LIGHTHOUSE—CIRCA 1950

Soon after Texas joined the Union, Matagorda Bay area was recognized as an important port, and Congress appropriated money for a lighthouse to be built at its entrance. Completed in 1852, the light shone out to sea for sixteen miles, guiding the merchant ships and military transports to safe harbor at Indianola and Lavaca.

At the beginning of the Civil War, Confederates attempted to dynamite the base of the lighthouse, and partially threw the tower over. The Union troops landed on Matagorda Island anyway and established a stronghold there, with 8,000 men and fourteen generals, until they were ordered back to New Orleans in 1864.

In 1867 the tower, heavily damaged by the dynamite and by sea erosion, was taken down, the plates were stored, and new plates were made to replace those damaged. It was rebuilt on the west side of Pass Cavallo, two miles away from its original setting.

The 1886 hurricane which totally destroyed Indianola also swept away all the buildings on the island except the tower and the keeper's house. But it rocked the tower so hard that a segment of the lens was jarred out and smashed onto the tower deck.

The U.S. Coast Guard dismantled and stored the lens in 1977, ending 123 years of lighthouse service. By then it was the only pre–Civil War lens still working on the Texas Gulf coast.

Apart from the tower, none of the buildings seen in this painting exist today. Only the magnificent, darkened tower remains, a lonely sentinel in Matagorda Island State Park. It still marks the pass between the bay and the Gulf, if only for shrimp boats and pleasure craft.

THE ARANSAS PASSAGE

Southwestward along the coast from ill-fated Matagorda Bay lie two smaller inlets, San Antonio Bay and Copano Bay. Fed by freshwater streams, the shallow bays support a diversity of wildlife in their diluted saline water and marshlands. Green plants such as diatoms, Indian grass, and yaupon feed larval crustaceans, grasshoppers, deer, and doves. Earthworms, ghost shrimp, and crabs provide food for cranes, raccoons, and gulls. Predators such as alligators, rattlesnakes, and bobcats prey upon the others. The land between the bays has intense and intricate *biotic communities*—where living organisms display a close interdependence.[1] Five miles offshore stand two barrier islands, Matagorda and San José (or Saint Joseph). Between the islands and the mainland run bodies of water connected to the Gulf of Mexico called Aransas Bay and Espiritu Santo Bay, and through that lagoon passes the Intracoastal Waterway on its way to Corpus Christi from Matagorda Bay. The Aransas National Wildlife Refuge occupies this mid-portion of the Texas coastline and its history is as significant and complex as the biotic communities it protects.

Although American attitudes about the land have generally affirmed exploitation for human benefit, concerns about the conservation and preservation of natural resources run deep into the American past. Giants such as Henry David Thoreau, George Perkins Marsh, John Wesley Powell, William Cullen Bryant, Frederick Law Olmsted, and John Muir spoke out in the nineteenth century, to be followed in the twentieth by Muir, Theodore Roosevelt, Gifford Pinchot, Aldo Leopold, and Franklin D. Roosevelt. The Audubon Society (founded in 1886), the Sierra Club (1892), the Izaak Walton League (1922), and the Wilderness Society (1935) boosted public awareness about conservation and agitated for protective legislation. Laws such as the Timber Culture Act (1873), the Forest Reserves Act (1891), and the National Park Service Act (1916) denoted increasing political recognition. Yellowstone National Park (1872), Yosemite National Park (1891), and fourteen others were already in existence by the time Congress created the National Park Service. The greatest boost for conservation, however, came with the Great Depression of the 1930s, when the dust bowl demonstrated the need for land preservation and the unemployment rate supplied labor for New Deal initiatives. It was this combination of awareness and opportunity that created the Aransas refuge.

An important role was played by the Audubon Society, whose early purpose was to protect birds by discouraging the use of feathers for fashionable decoration. But there was also a national demand on restaurant menus for wild game, especially waterfowl, which reached Texas when refrigerated transportation became available in the 1870s. About sixty species supplied the market.[2] The central Texas coast, as it turned out, was in the middle of a central flyway for migrating birds, and avian life was abundant. Traveling eastward by boat along this coast in January 1853, John Russell Bartlett, a member of the United States and Mexican Boundary Commission, observed:

Our course lay through a channel less than twenty yards wide for miles, with bars of sand on both sides but an inch or two above the water. These were covered with myriads of water-fowl, including cranes, swans, herons, ibises, geese, ducks, curlews, plover, sandpipers, etc. The large cranes and swans stood in lines extending for miles, appearing like a light sandy beach or white cliff; and it was impossible to dispel the delusion, until the vast flock, with a simultaneous scream that could be heard for miles, rose from their resting place. Occasionally, we would round a point which concealed a bay the surface of which was filled with ducks and geese; these, taking the alarm, would rise in one continuous flock, making a noise like thunder, as they flapped their wings on emerging from the water.[3]

By the turn of the century the numbers of nesting waterbirds were dwindling and the Texas chapter of the Audubon Society, established in 1899, was successful in 1903 in obtaining a state law making it illegal to hunt wild species for profit. Sportsmen, however, could still bag twenty-five ducks per gun per day, and there was no warden to enforce the statute. Game was still being illegally shipped to St. Louis and Chicago. The society then set up local organizations and appealed to educators, women's clubs, and politicians. A revision in 1907 required the sale of hunting licenses to provide the money necessary for the Game, Fish and Oyster Commission to enforce the law. T. Gilbert Pearson of the National Audubon Society, moreover, surveyed the Texas coast in 1918, and did so again in 1920, looking for nesting sites to protect. He noted the rookeries of San Antonio Bay and the islands of Laguna Madre south of Corpus Christi. The Texas legislature released three of these islands to the protection of the Audubon Society in 1921 at no cost. In 1925, in addition, the state encouraged landowners to establish private game preserves, which resulted in fifty-three such places in the 1930s.[4]

The federal government, meanwhile, began establishing migratory bird refuges as habitats for ducks and geese along the central flyway to the coastal wetlands. These were financed by the Migratory Bird Hunting Stamp Act in 1934. An earlier enactment with Great Britain (Canada) in 1918, the Migratory Bird Treaty Act, produced a recommendation by the Bureau of Biological Survey to buy the St. Charles Ranch on the Texas Coast where bureau ornithologist George B. Saunders had spotted several whooping cranes. Federal money thus purchased the tidal marshes of the ranch on the Blackjack Peninsula for the Aransas National Wildlife Refuge in 1937. The Civilian Conservation Corps of the New Deal built the first roads, levees, and houses, and the concrete base of their flagpole remains as a memorial. The sanctuary later expanded with additions of adjoining property, including Matagorda Island, an offshore sand-barrier isle. This island, too, has a complex history.

Following the devastating hurricanes of 1876 and 1886, there was little commercial promise left for either Matagorda Bay or Matagorda Island. The lighthouse on the island, however, survived as a symbol of a violent past. Originally authorized by the U.S. government in 1847, the cast-iron tower was erected in 1852 by Murray and Hazelhurst of Boston. It became the first operating lighthouse on the Texas coast. The tower, raised from fifty-five to seventy-nine feet in 1859, had horizontal red, white, and black stripes and a flashing light that could be seen sixteen miles out at sea. The lighthouse was damaged during the Civil War, but it was reworked, painted solid black, and rebuilt on a higher location in 1873. It was improved over time so that its light could be seen for forty-five miles. Finally, in 1977, it ceased its duty as a lighthouse, but the Coast Guard maintained it for the National Registry of Historic Landmarks. It now casts a weaker beam, visible for eighteen miles, and serves as a visiting site for painters and day-hikers.

Ranchers, taking advantage of a range confined by water, took over the unused island in the last part of the nineteenth century. Between 1933 and 1941, oilman Clint Murchison bought the southern nine miles of the thirty-eight-mile isle which he leased to the federal government for one dollar per year at the outbreak of World War II. The government purchased the remainder of the island from other ranchers for a wartime gunnery range. Until 1960 the mid-portion was pounded with all sorts of aerial bombs and strafing bullets as young fighter pilots learned their craft. Following this, Matagorda Island became a hunting and fishing reserve for officers, until it was closed in 1978 as a military facility.

The federal government gave its land to the Aransas refuge, while the state, which owned the beaches and tidal flats, set up Matagorda Island State Park and Wildlife Management Area. Meanwhile, Toddie Lee Wynne became owner of the southern portion after a partnership fallout with Clint Murchison. Wynne continued to operate a ranch and used the island twice as a launching pad for private space rockets. Wynne died of a heart attack in 1982, however, and the Texas Nature Conservancy, a conservation organization, bought the property. The Nature Conservancy turned the land over to the U.S. Department of Interior, and thus in 1988 Matagorda Island became the only barrier island in Texas under public control. With its black lighthouse standing guard, it has remained a state park and wildlife refuge with public access only by boat from Port O'Conner.[5]

Birds flocked to both sides of the lagoon, but as might be expected, the diversity of avian life was greater on the mainland due to the greater feeding capacity of the land compared with that of a sand island. After the passage of the federal Endangered Species Act in 1973, about three dozen species of animals found protection at Aransas, including the brown pelican, Attwater's greater

ARANSAS NATIONAL WILDLIFE REFUGE

In early April of each year, the sound of wild trumpeting can be heard throughout the marshland of south Texas and with that sound, whooping cranes stretch their wings and slowly spiral upward. This begins their 2,500-mile semi-annual journey that takes them to their nesting grounds in northern Canada and back again to Texas in the fall. Whooping cranes are unique to North America, and stand nearly five feet tall, with a wing span of 7-1/2 feet, making them the largest bird natural to this continent. Whooping cranes mate for life and usually lay two eggs, though they rarely raise more than one chick. Each family occupies a very large area or territory in the refuge and protects it from other whooping cranes. Food is abundant in this peaceful isolation, where they feed on blue crabs, worms, clams, small marine life, and the occasional small fish.

In 1937 the Aransas National Wildlife Refuge was created to protect these beautiful birds from extinction. Only 18 could be accounted for in 1938, but by 1989 there were approximately 150. The struggle to protect these magnificent creatures by the Department of Interior is thus having very positive results.

The refuge is also home to an abundance of other wildlife. Mild winters and ample food supply attract over 389 bird species, and it is a haven for reptiles, including alligators, turtles, frogs, and snakes. Dense thickets provide shelter for deer, javelina, coyote, bobcat, and other mammals. And this place can also be viewed as a refuge for people who enjoy observing wildlife and plants.

The Aransas National Wildlife Refuge is one of eight national bird and wildlife sanctuaries located along the Gulf coast. There are, in addition to the eight on the coast, sanctuaries on Padre Island National Seashore.

FULTON MANSION—FULTON BEACH

George Fulton came to Texas from Philadelphia in 1837. Arriving too late to fight for independence, he set about locating and patenting land claims, concentrating on the Live Oak peninsula in Refugio County. He married the daughter of a business associate, moved to Baltimore to raise a family, and returned to Texas after the Civil War to raise cattle. Buoyed by the bright prospects of the cattle business, the Fultons began construction of "Oakhurst," as they called their new mansion. In 1877 they moved into their new home, which was filled with the latest gadgets and Mr. Fulton's inventions. This house boasted a gas plant to supply fuel for gaslight chandeliers and cisterns in the basement for an adequate water supply. A tank in the attic provided gravity-fed water to bathrooms, complete with flush toilets and bathtubs. The house was heated and ventilated through ducts and flues, and hot air was also piped into the basement laundry room to dry clothes hung on wooden racks. There was a dumb waiter and, in the larder, water circulated through troughs to cool perishable food.

While many people recognize this mansion from the front—that is, the waterfront side, the artist chose to paint the back of the house, as most of the activities of the family took place there under the shade of the oaks. There, the grandchildren played games while their mothers tended the rose and vegetable gardens and Mrs. Fulton observed her happy brood from her porch.

When George Fulton died, the house underwent numerous changes in ownership and suffered serious deterioration until it was purchased and restored by the Texas Parks and Wildlife Department. The mansion is preserved as a museum and is open to the public.

prairie chicken, the southern bald eagle, the jaguarundi, and alligators. The most significant in terms of popularity, however, was the whooping crane, which became a symbol of the conservation movement. It was a bird admired for its beauty, dignity, independence, and tenacity. It was also a threatened species which managed to survive with human help.

Whooping cranes are the tallest birds in North America, the male standing almost five feet high, with a wingspan of seven-and-a-half feet. The female is slightly smaller. They have white glossy feathers with black wing tips which show only in flight, long curved necks, bulky bodies, long black legs, large, strong beaks surrounded by black feathers, a crown of red skin, and fierce yellow eyes. They mate for life, live about twenty-five years, migrate 2,500 miles in about thirty days to northern Canada for summer breeding, and associate in family groups that require about 300 acres of tidal land. The cranes eat clams, marine worms, insects, snails, fish, frogs, snakes, mice, grass, and acorns. Their favorite food is the blue crab. An adult pair, bowing and leaping, will also spontaneously dance with each other. They chase other birds from their territory, bugle warnings, and are very cautious.[6] When Frederick Law Olmsted first saw whoopers in 1854 near Austin, he thought that they were sheep.

While riding slowly, we saw some white objects on a hill before us. We could not make them out distinctly, and resorted to the spy-glass. "Sheep," said one. "Cattle," said the other. As we rode on, we slowly approached. "Yes, sheep," said one. "Decidedly not sheep," said the other. Suddenly, one of the objects raises a long neck and head. "Llamas—or alpacas." "More like birds, I think." Then all the objects raise heads, and begin to walk away, upon two legs. "What! ostriches? Yes, ostriches, or something unknown to my eye." We were now within four or five hundred yards of them. Suddenly, they raised wings, stretched out their necks, and ran over the prairie, but presently left ground, and flew away. They were very large white birds, with black-edged wings, and very long necks and legs. They must have been a species of crane, very much magnified by a refraction of the atmosphere.[7]

In Manitoba, Canada, they were referred to as "flying sheep," and it was a Canadian, Fred Bard of the Provincial Museum in Regina, Saskatchewan, who first searched for the northern nesting grounds in 1945 under the auspices of the Audubon Society. The society was curious about the migration pattern and Olin Pettingill Jr., an ornithologist, took up the quest in 1946. When Pettingill left for teaching duties at Carleton College the mystery was turned over to Robert P. Allen, the research director of the National Audubon Society. He became the whoopers' greatest champion.

Allen visited the Blackjack Peninsula, made bird counts, and helped change local attitudes. At the gatherings in the general store in Austwell, Texas, the nearest town to Aransas, the typical conversation had been: "I hear the government is buying up the Blackjacks for a pile of money just to protect a couple of them squawking cranes! They tell me they ain't bad eating, but there's no open season on them. . . . If you can't shoot them, what the blankety-blank good are they?"[8] A local rancher once assured the first manager of the refuge that he only shot whoopers for eating and never "more than one every week or so."[9] In time, Cap Daniel, the owner of the store in Austwell, asked Allen for pictures of the cranes. Daniel then removed from the wall a picture of western independence, Judge Roy Bean and the "Law West of the Pecos," and replaced it with Allen's pictures.[10] This was a triumph for Allen and the Aransas refuge.

Allen's research report to the Audubon Society, *The Whooping Crane: Research Report 3*, in 1952 is considered one of the classics of wildlife research, but the migration pattern remained elusive. In April or so, every year, Allen observed the birds at Aransas becoming restless. They at last leaped into the air, spiraled upward to catch favorable winds to the north, and disappeared. In October they returned, dropping from the sky exhausted and hungry, often with a young bird trailing. It was a migration pattern taught by the older birds; it was not instinct. Allen flew some twenty thousand miles searching for the nests and helped publicize the quest.

In late June 1954 a forest fire in a remote area of Wood Buffalo National Park in the Northwest Territories of Canada ended the search. Two Canadian wildlife officers in a helicopter investigating the fire spotted two large white birds two miles from the blaze. Flying lower, they spotted not only whooping cranes, but also a rust-colored juvenile about the size of a rooster. Ground investigations of the tangled marshland confirmed the summer nesting site.[11] The migration mystery was solved. The problem remained, however, of how to protect the whoopers from the hazards of a long journey and of how to safeguard its habitats.

According to Allen, there were never many whooping cranes—perhaps only 1,500, with a wide range. A non-migrating group of eleven birds survived in Louisiana until the opening of their secret lake by the Intracoastal Waterway in 1929. This colony was down to a single member by 1947. At Aransas in 1938 the first supervisor counted eighteen cranes. Then the engineers of the Intracoastal Waterway in 1940 cut through the salt flats of the refuge, destroying not only habitat, but also isolation. Barges began to chug through the sanctuary, and when the gunnery range at Matagorda Island opened, student pilots dove at geese and large birds. Rights to drill for oil had been retained by the earlier property owners and in 1941 while James O. Stevenson, the first manager, and Robert Allen watched, barges attending a well discharged oil suddenly into the water. Helplessly they looked on as the slick spread toward the canal, where it would wash into the mud flats of the refuge. It threatened to bring death to the plants and migrating whoopers, but a shift in the wind forestalled disaster.[12] Life for birds at the "refuge" was precarious indeed.

Despite bombs, barges, oil wells, and errant hunters, the whooping cranes returned annually to Aransas and maintained their tenacious hold on life. Numbers of birds slowly increased over time—there were 34 in 1950, 36 in 1960, 56 in 1970, 76 in 1980, 146 in 1990, and 158 in 1996. The bombing at Matagorda ended, but the possibility of a calamitous oil or chemical spill in the refuge continued as a never-ending nightmare. The natural watercourse between Matagorda and San José islands, for in-

stance, was deliberately plugged in 1979 to protect the lagoon from the massive Ixtoc oil spill in Mexico.

The barges on the Intracoastal Waterway not only carried toxic products through the refuge, they also washed away precious soil with their waves. Rerouting the canal seemed no solution and very expensive. So the Corps of Engineers continued its dredging and piling up of spoil banks. Although it was observed early on that the spoil provided nesting ground for a variety of seabirds, the channel was too deep for cranes to wade. After losing about twenty feet of shoreline per year to the Intracoastal Waterway with its constant shoaling, in 1992 the Corps finally reinforced critical embankments with concrete mats. Recently, Mitchell Energy Company of Houston, with the cooperation of the refuge, successfully constructed crane islands from dredged materials, complete with vegetation. It would have cost the company more money to haul the spoil away from their natural gas wells than it did to build the new area. "It's a win-win situation," said President George P. Mitchell. "We had material to dispose of and the whooping cranes needed more habitat." Tom Stehn, the refuge biologist, thinks now that the problem of habitat loss may have been solved by the company's effort.[13]

To offset the possibility of a disaster that might destroy the Aransas refuge, aviculturists experimented with captive propagation of whooping cranes at the Patuxent Wildlife Research Center in Laural, Maryland, and with the establishment of a second colony at Grays Lake, Idaho. The release of captive cranes at Grays Lake in the 1970s proved a failure when the cranes refused to breed, but the idea of establishing a second flock did not die. Captive whoopers were released in Florida through the 1990s, with the hopes of starting a non-migrating colony.

It might be argued that the effort of conservation at Aransas was as important for humanity as it was for the endangered species on the coast. After all, about eighty percent of North America's migratory birds travel through the Aransas refuge every year. As Richard C. Bartlett, chairman of the Nature Conservancy of Texas, commented about the sanctuary in 1995, "This is the defensive base camp for most of North America's migratory birds, the core that must be defended if our continent is to have

ARANSAS PASS LIGHTHOUSE

The tides are in, the egrets are fishing for their meal, and the tower stands sentinel over Aransas Pass as it has done for more than 140 years. To those privileged to visit this place there is an awareness that the walls speak if one listens carefully. They speak of their beginning, when the U.S. Lighthouse Service (which had been instituted long ago by Benjamin Franklin) appropriated funds for a light at Harbor Island on the coast of Texas. They speak, too, of the damage done by both Confederate and Union forces. The Confederates removed the light, buried it, and blew up the top of the tower. The Union forces used it for target practice. The walls speak of hurricanes and people whose lives were saved when they sought refuge in the tower, and of people who cared for and lovingly restored the historical sites.

The lighthouse marked the Corpus Christi bayou two miles south, where ships could be guided through to safe harbor. In the early part of this century, the U.S. Corps of Engineers Jetty Project built a new ship channel and the light became less important. Then, in 1952, the Coast Guard closed down the lighthouse, moved to Port Aransas, and erected a much taller light at the new station. Shortly after, the Aransas Pass lighthouse was declared surplus and was offered for sale. The present owner has gone to considerable expense to put this historic site in a good state of repair, and relighted the tower on July 4, 1988. The old tower has since returned to duty, and is recognized by the Coast Guard as an official aid to navigation.

Of particular note is the story of the storm of 1916. The keeper, Frank Stevenson, together with his daughter and son-in-law and their children, sought safety from the storm in the tower, which became flooded over the door. There, they endured sixteen hours of horror and for two weeks lived in the tower, until help came. The tower was all that was left standing, and Frank Stevenson vowed that he would rebuild the house, making it so strong that it could withstand any storm. In 1917 he began construction. To ensure its durability, the foundation was made of cast-iron pilings buried deep into the ground. He used double-planked diagonal floors and tongue-and-groove roof decking one inch thick and cross-pined with copper, and all of the wood was long-leaf pine. When an even stronger storm hit in 1919, this dwelling rode it out with practically no damage. It was as though Frank Stevenson was shaking his fist at the storm and saying, "I bested you!"

birdlife."[14] Where would Texas and the nation be without such birds? Certainly our lives would be diminished in terms of beauty and song, and considerably overridden with bugs. But the Aransas story also tells something about human beings—the only species of the planet to develop conscious concern about the welfare of another species. Consider the change since George B. Sennett, a renowned ornithologist, was collecting whooping crane eggs in 1876. Sennett had hidden near a nest when the female bird returned and settled on the eggs.

I could see her wink her eyes, watching me and her mate constantly. Her eyes gleamed like fire. How anxious and how handsome, was ever a sight so grand! The male stood on the ridge watching her closely for a few minutes, when, feeling all was safe he calmly commenced to plume himself in grand style and shortly walked off away from me, the proudest of birds. I slowly arose, turned, and gave her one barrel as she was rising from the nest and the next before she had gone six feet and dropped her in the water.[15]

Even John James Audubon killed the specimens he painted so magnificently in the nineteenth century. It is not so now. Human beings have traveled far as pilgrims on the road of conservation and compassion. The Aransas history is a part of that change.

CORPUS CHRISTI

AND THE COWTOWNS OF THE COAST

The name "Corpus Christi," the body of Christ, commemorates the culture of the first European explorers, as do other names along the Texas coast. Alonso Alvarez de Piñeda, according to legend, sighted and named the bay on Corpus Christi Day in 1519 when he claimed the area for the Spanish crown, but Diego Ortiz Parrilla provided the first historical reference in his 1767 report about the South Texas coast. Although Blas María de la Garza Falcón established a ranching outpost in what is now Nueces County, there was little settlement activity in the area until potential warfare brought an American army to the west side of Corpus Christi Bay in 1845. And this was temporary, a brief noisy human episode disturbing the quiet of the coastal bend.

Fired by what later became known as "Manifest Destiny," President James K. Polk sent General Zachary Taylor with nearly half of the U.S. Army to protect the new state of Texas from Mexico. Sailing from New Orleans, the soldiers first landed on San José Island, and shortly jumped to a camp on what later became North Beach in Corpus Christi. The encampment site is now the location of the Texas State Aquarium. The 3,000 soldiers lived on the shore, fought the rattlesnakes—they killed 114 the second day—fished, held horseback races on the sand, and suffered from dysentery, since their latrines were uphill from their shallow drinking wells. They stayed for seven months, along with some 1,000 camp followers, who provided gambling, entertainment, and other services. "There are no ladies here," recorded Lieutenant Colonel Eathan Allen Hitchcock, "and very few women."[1]

Nearby, on the high bluff overlooking the camp, Henry L. Kinney and William P. Aubrey had established a frontier trading post in 1839. It gave Texas a claim to the Nueces strip, and at this uncertain boundary of politics and culture the post provided an exchange point for contraband and ideas between Mexicans, Americans, and Indians. Said Kinney, "When Mr. Mexican came, I treated him with a great deal of politeness, particularly if he had me in his power. When Mr. American came, I did the same with him, and when Mr. Indian came, I was also very fre-

quently disposed to make a compromise with him."[2] When, in March 1846, Taylor marched away to military glory at the battles of Resaca de la Palma and Buena Vista on the Rio Grande, he left Kinney with a residue of civilians and a vestigial town.

The resourceful Kinney, who had been a senator in the Republic of Texas, was reelected to the first four legislatures of the new state. He played a minor role in the war, bought land, and tried to promote Corpus Christi as "The Naples of the Gulf." Kinney organized a grand fair in 1852, with $3,000 in prizes, in order to attract attention. He imported a carnival from New Orleans, staged bull fights, and offered a warehouse of Mexican trade goods. Ashbel Smith, the master of ceremonies, declared the fair a success, but Kinney lost money and went into debt. He tried to recover with fanciful real-estate manipulations in Nicaragua, but failed. Returning to Texas, Kinney won election to the Texas Legislature again in 1858, but resigned because he disagreed with the Texas decision for secession. He retired to Matamoros, offered to help both sides in the Civil War, and apparently died on March 3, 1862, from a gunshot at 3:00 A.M. There is only a sketchy record of his death, but the implication is that Kinney, who had a roving eye, met his end at the hand of a jealous husband.[3]

Be that as it may, Kinney's efforts to promote Corpus Christi were by and large a failure. The town was too remote and, as General Taylor discovered, mud flats and a sandbar blocked the bay. The Nueces River, thought by Mexico to be the boundary of the Republic of Texas, empties into a saltwater estuary that joins Corpus Christi Bay. Mustang Island, part of the sand-barrier chain, protects the open mouth of the bay from the Gulf of Mexico. Mustang is located southwest of San José and Matagorda islands, where the coastal shore of Texas turns almost due south. Aransas Bay to the northeast and Laguna Madre to the south make up the shallow lagoons between the mainland and the barrier islands. Corpus Christi Bay, twenty-one miles wide, offered an opportunity for a fairly secure harbor, but there was little economic need for one there until the opening of the Texas cattle frontier.

CORPUS CHRISTI REVISITED

Corpus Christi is, to many, their favorite city on the Gulf coast. The ships, the aquarium, the beautiful seashore, and the delicious seafood can sometimes make one forget that Corpus Christi also has an interesting past. Sitting quietly on the steps of the seawall, through the spray of the surf, one can imagine Alonso Alvarez de Piñeda, who, according to legend, on Corpus Christi Day in 1519, named the bay for the day. Or perhaps another ghost might appear in the uniform of a soldier from the Mexican War. He, too, came to Corpus Christi with General Zachary Taylor and three thousand men who camped there for seven months before marching toward Mexico.

Corpus Christi remained a small village until this century, when it found prosperity in the form of oil refineries, shipping, and tourism. When one visits Corpus Christi today, one is struck by the beauty of the shoreline, graced by the pure white miradores (gazebos) embracing the seawall. Seven miradores have been placed there by Dusty Durrill in memory of his daughter, Debry, who was killed in an auto accident. In May 1997 an eighth mirador was placed by the Durrill Foundation and dedicated to the memory of Selena, the popular Hispanic singer. Her statue stands in the center of her mirador. And as we sit on the steps of the seawall, if we listen carefully we might just hear her singing in the music of the surf as she, too, revisits her "Sparkling City by the Sea."

The interior coastal country was mainly flat grassland with about twenty-seven inches of rainfall per year—dry, but not arid. It was slightly beyond the reach of southern cotton cultivation, and ideal for livestock. The Spanish brought in the first cattle and over time the Spanish cows developed into the multi-colored, slab-sided Texas longhorns noted for their ability to live on sparse rations and to fend for themselves. During the Civil War, with few men to tend them, the herds multiplied, and afterward a Texas cow, worth four dollars in South Texas, was valued at ten times that amount in the cattle towns of Kansas. Fortunes could be made in rounding up longhorns and driving them northward. The Nueces river valley was thus the cradle of the cattle frontier, and remained so for about two decades, from 1865 to 1885. This was the time of cowboys, Indians, the Chisholm Trail, Dodge City, and cattle barons along the South Texas coast.

The long drive north was filled with hazards of drought, stampedes, grass fires, Indian raids, and river crossings. Such adventures provided the foundation for western American culture—history, novels, poetry, music—but economically, it made sense to investigate other routes to markets and profit. Thus, Corpus Christi, Rockport, and Fulton became cattle towns on the coast. Rockport, named for a rock ledge under its shoreline, began with cattle pens, packeries, and a dock built between 1865 and 1868. W. S. Hall, the first packer in Texas, processed 11,000 cows per year into tallow for soap and candles, horns for buttons and combs, hides for leather, bones for fertilizer, and choice pieces of meat for Boston Canned Beef. Waste was fed to hogs or dumped into the bay. The families of Thomas H. Mathis, George Ware Fulton, and Youngs Coleman formed a land-cattle-packing partnership that controlled 115,000 acres and brought a boom time to the small port. In 1884 the company helped to promote the million-dollar San Antonio and Aransas Pass Railway (SA&AP) to bring cattle to the coast, but unfortunately, at the same time, the Morgan Shipping Lines withdrew its shallow-draft steamships. The cattle frontier ended, ranchers shipped cows by rail to the market, the Coleman-Fulton Pasture Company sold its

pens, wharf, and warehouses, the railroad went bankrupt in 1890, and Rockport's growth days were over.[4]

Fulton, a related cattle town on Aransas Bay named for George Ware Fulton, one of the partners, suffered the same fate—boom and bust. As the meat packers closed, some switched from cows to turtles. They kept their captured sea turtles swimming in large sea-water pens until their fate was ordered. This lasted until the turn of the century. What was then left for the future of Fulton and Rockport was a small fishing industry, and tourism based upon beach activities, sport fishing, and bird watching. At Rockport, for example, Martha Conger "Connie" Hagar counted birds in a four-by-seven-mile tract twice a day for thirty-five years starting in 1935. She discovered among the 400 or so species that visited the area nine different sorts of hummingbirds and compiled an authoritative checklist of birds for the central Texas coast. To a large extent, Rockport, which was only thirty-five miles from the Aransas refuge, became the bird-watcher's mecca of the United States through her efforts.[5]

George Ware Fulton also left his mark three miles north of Rockport between 1874 and 1877 by building a twenty-nine-room, three-story mansion facing Aransas Bay. The home had gas lighting, central heat, flush toilets, and a larder cooled by water in the basement. It was a marvel of its time and was well used by the Fulton family and children into the 1890s. The house survived neglect and storms and was restored in 1976 by the Texas Parks and Wildlife Department. Mansions of the same sort, produced by the wealth of the cattle frontier, also appeared on the bluff at Corpus Christi. Most of these mansions, however, have disappeared in the expansion of the city. The last one remaining, Centennial House, was also the earliest. Forbes Britton, a merchant and rancher who had fought alongside Taylor in Mexico, bought the site from Kinney and built the shellcrete (pulverized oyster shells baked into bricks) Greek-revival-style home in 1849. It served as a hospital after the Civil War, became an office, and then, after 1965, survived as a tourist site preserved by the Corpus Christi Heritage Society.

Corpus Christi, meanwhile, suffered through the inflation and deflation resulting from the activities of a town promoter, Colonel Elihu H. Ropes. After a visit to Galveston, this magnetic and flamboyant former advertising manager for the Singer Sewing Machine Company from New Jersey decided to develop Corpus Christi as a deep-water port in 1888 and 1889. He organized the Port Ropes Company, attracted capital, purchased Mustang Island, hired a dredge to cut through the island, built the 125-room Alta Vista Hotel, and dreamed of a railroad from Corpus Christi to South America. He was caught, however, in the financial panic of 1893, left town with his secretary, Miss Woodcock, and never returned. The grand Alta Vista Hotel never opened, the ship channel remained undredged, and the population, which had doubled in numbers, receded almost to where it had been before Ropes. The only lasting accomplishment was a new water supply system.[6]

Railroad agents in the next decade, however, promoted the area and modernization took place under progressive Mayor Roy Miller. The city paved its streets, built a new city hall, laid storm drains, established a professional fire department, and sold bonds to improve the slope up the "bald and unsightly" bluff with stairs, roads, and a fountain. Tourists arrived, including, in 1909, President William H. Taft, whose brother owned a nearby ranch. In 1913, across the bay at White Point, a natural gas well blew in and blew up. The explosion rocked the folks at Corpus Christi and the fire lighted the sky for months. Although the first producing well was not drilled for another ten years, the gas well and later oil wells gave the area an economic punch. Corpus Christi developed into the nation's third largest petrochemical complex, with refineries sitting cheek by jowl with homes within the city limits. More trouble with Mexico, meanwhile, brought the Texas National Guard to Camp Scurry at Corpus Christi and World War I kept the encampment in operation.[7]

It all added up to growth and a need for a deep-water harbor at Corpus Christi. Transferring shipments at Rockport, which was none too deep itself, for lightering across the sandbars into Cor-

pus Christi Bay was no longer acceptable. Representative John Nance Garner of Uvalde was able to get Corpus Christi Bay included in the 1907 Rivers and Harbors Bill for a small amount. This was a first step, and investigation by the Corps of Engineers began, but progress was slow and shoaling posed a problem. Then, in 1919, a hurricane struck with 110-mile-per-hour winds. People had been warned to escape, but an eleven-foot tidal surge pounded the lower tier of the city up to the bluff and swept away the tourist cottages at North Beach. As the twenty-four-hour storm receded it left between 350 and 400 people dead in the wet wreckage and $20 million in damage.[8] It was a pivotal point for the town's future.

The people wanted protection and the state donated the ad valorem taxes of six counties for twenty-five years for a seawall and breakwater. In 1922 the city, meanwhile, competed with Rockport and Aransas Pass for deep-water designation by the federal government. Corpus Christi won because it had more railroads. Roy Miller, who helped lead a committee of business leaders, waited two hours outside the speaker's house in Washington, D.C. with a taxi meter running in order to get an appropriation inserted into the Rivers and Harbor Bill. The Corps of Engineers insisted, however, that the breakwater come first in order to protect the harbor the engineers would dredge. This was done, the tax money was spent, and a wide curve of granite blocks was dumped into the sea. The engineers opened a twenty-five-foot-deep harbor and ship channel through the bay in 1926 and subsequently deepened it as needed. Following the 1919 hurricane the population dropped by one-third, to 9,000 people. With the opening of the port, the population tripled to 28,000 by 1930.[9] The city had succeeded and the Deep Water Committee formed by the leaders had won.

There remained the question of individual protection. The people themselves were still at the mercy of the sea and they wanted a seawall. By the end of the 1930s property evaluations were high enough to support the sale of bonds to pay for a project. The result was a concrete wall with a stairstep configuration,

BROADWAY-CORPUS CHRISTI
"AFTERNOON CALL AT
MRS HENRIETTA KING'S HOME"

A VISIT WITH MRS. HENRIETTA KING

Built in 1893 by Mrs. Henrietta King, the widow of Richard King of King Ranch, this home served as a place where Mrs. King could enjoy the summer breezes off the Corpus Christi Bay and from which some of her grandchildren attended school. It was situated on the bluff above the town of Corpus Christi on a street later named Upper Broadway. To the south were the homes of longtime friends and business associates John Kenedy, Jr., and Mifflin Kenedy. Mrs. King requested architect James Riley Gordon to make the home a comfortable one without being ornate. Although Henrietta King was raised in modest circumstances and became one of the wealthiest women in the world, she never seemed dazzled by the things her money could buy. In fact, she was diligent and philanthropic in the way she used her money and power.

The first of Mrs. King's many gifts was made to Corpus Christi: In 1900 she granted the land and money to build the area's first modern hospital. A year later she gave land and funds to the First Presbyterian Church of Corpus Christi. Later, she realized a dream of her husband by creating the city of Kingsville, complete with institutions of learning, libraries, and land for churches of every denomination.

Because of her business acumen, her philanthropic ways, and her deep religious commitments, all of which showed through her quiet demeanor, she has been affectionately known, by both famous and ordinary people, as "Mamacita of South Texas."

12,000 feet long and fourteen feet above sea level. Fill land in front of the city, together with T-head piers and three boat basins, were a part of the construction. It was completed in 1941, twenty-two years after the great storm.[10]

During the 1930s and into the war years refineries came to the bay area, as well as the U.S. Navy. Looking for a seaplane base, the navy sent a survey team there in 1938. With encouragement from congressional representatives and donations by Corpus Christi of roads, water, and housing, a $53-million naval air station opened in 1941. During the war it became the city's largest employer, and afterwards Corpus Christi worked to hold onto the base while expanding its tourist trade. Tourists, of course, had come to Corpus Christi since the time of Kinney's ill-conceived fair. Railroads brought more travelers, and North Beach developed as a resort area at the turn of the century. Bathhouses for sea bathing, piers for fishing, and a hotel were built. Boxer Bob Fitzsimmons, with a pet lion that slept under his cottage, trained at North Beach for his professional boxing match with "Gentleman" Jim Corbett. Fitzsimmons lost the match. The Methodist Church built "Epworth by the Sea" at North Beach as a religious retreat. All was swept away except the Beach Hotel, however, in the hurricane of 1919.[11]

In the 1920s, theater entrepreneur Bruce Collins rebuilt the area as "The Playground of the South," with a roller coaster, a dance pavilion, and a saltwater swimming pool fenced to keep out the jellyfish. He introduced "Splash Day" beauty contests to open the summer season, hosted speedboat races, and staged marathon dance competitions.[12] For journalist Bill Walraven, the area became a fond memory:

A trip to North Beach was like Christmas and Thanksgiving all in one, under the palm trees on the soft warm sand. It was long remembered—the cool afternoon breezes, the cries of the laughing gulls, brown pelicans perched silently on each piling, and the sound of the wind whipping through the tall palms at the water's edge in front of the bathhouse, mingled with the music and screams from the carnival. Half a century later I am still transfixed by that bay. I can still sit and look at it for hours, still feeling some of that childhood happiness.[13]

Damaged by storms, beach erosion, the opening of Padre Island, and harbor bridges which isolated the area, North Beach declined. Its revival came not as a beach, but as a tourist destination for visitors to the Texas State Aquarium in 1990 and to the retired aircraft carrier, *Lexington*, in 1992. Across the channel the Columbian replica ships *Nina*, *Pinta*, and *Santa Maria* have been docked since 1993. These three major attractions, even though they have no direct historical connection with the city, emphasize Corpus Christi's link to the sea and, most important, indicate its commitment to tourism as an important element in the economy. In 1988 Mayor Betty Turner commented that tourism was the "only hope for economic recovery." This was a time of economic doldrums for Texas and the tourist trade was the biggest industry that could be tapped in the shortest amount of time.[14]

Tourism was not a new song for Corpus Christi, but there were changes in the tune. During the 1920s and 1930s the Chamber of Commerce advertised the city as "Where Texas Meets the Sea" and in the 1980s the Convention and Tourist Bureau boosted the "Sparkling City by the Sea." The bureau now advertises, in addition, "Gateway to Padre Island National Seashore." Access by tourists to this long barrier island influences the contemporary history of Corpus Christi and shifts the economic emphasis of the South Texas coast. Padre Island, like other places along the Texas coastline, has a story to tell about hurricanes, shipwrecks, conservation, business, tourism, and redemption of the human spirit.

PADRE ISLAND

SHIPWRECKS AND TOURISTS

Eastward from Corpus Christi and across a causeway lies the northern tip of Padre Island. It is the longest sand-barrier island in the world, stretching for 130 miles, and it parallels the coast from Corpus Christi Bay southward almost to the Rio Grande border with Mexico. It is three miles wide, bright, sandy, hot, windswept, and the home of kangaroo rats, rattlesnakes, coyotes, and blacktail jackrabbits. The thirty-five-foot-high dunes and back areas support some 600 species of plants and wildflowers, but there is little shade or fresh water. Ducks and other waterfowl crowd the marsh borders of Laguna Madre, the shallow, green-colored "mother lagoon" that separates the island from the mainland. About midway down the island is Big Shell, where churning offshore currents create upon the beach a shell hunter's paradise, one of the best in the United States. The curve of the shoreline, the agitation in the currents, and the unsettled air prone to storms have made this part of Padre Island not only a depository for shells, but also a graveyard for wrecked ships. For a traveler or tourist, Padre Island therefore promises an adventure linked to the shore and the sea. The exposed, dehydrating environment, however, has the effect of shortening ambitious excursions to a few hours.

The island was officially explored by José Antonio de la Garza Falcón in 1766 as a part of the coastal survey by Diego Ortiz Parrilla. The viceroy of New Spain ordered an investigation because of rumors concerning English squatters on the "Islas Blancas," the barrier islands. Riding down the beach on horseback, Garza Falcón and his men found rigging, masts, spars, and other nautical debris. On Brazos Island, at the mouth of the Rio Grande, they found the hulk of a twenty-gun English ship, but no intruders. The map submitted by Ortiz Parrilla as a part of his report was fairly accurate and indicated the extent of what became known as Padre Island at a later time. The island, however, had already acquired a notorious reputation, due to the wreck there of a treasure fleet in 1554.

Carrying gold, silver bullion, cochineal (red dye), cowhides, resins, and 410 people, including crew members, the *Santa María de Yciar*, the *San Esteban*, the *San Andres*, and *the Espíritu Santo* left Veracruz for Spain in April of that year. Caught by a storm, probably not a hurricane, three of the ships ran aground and burst apart on Padre Island; only the battered *San Andres*, with 106 people, escaped to Havana. Along with crates of food—biscuit, meat, and fruit jelly—floated by the waves from the shattered ships, the majority of the passengers and crew made it to shore—probably about 200 people. A small boat with some of the survivors may have successfully returned to Veracruz, or to Tampico. The rest chose to walk back, but only two lived through the ordeal.

According to Fray Marcos de Mena, one of the survivors who related his story thirty years later, after staying at the wreck site for five to six days the castaways, including women and children, began a trek down the island to Pánuco in Mexico. After seven days' march they were accosted by armed Indians, who feigned peace by offering food and then attacked. The Spaniards marched on, harassed by the Indians, who picked off stragglers. Their clothes fell apart, their shoes wore out, food became short, and they lost their only weapons, two crossbows, while crossing a river. Noting that the Indians stripped two Spanish captives of their clothing and then left the men unharmed, the main group disrobed and left their clothes to the natives. It did no good, however, and Indian bands continued to chase and kill them on their southerly trek. The survivors crossed the Rio Grande, divided into struggling groups, and one by one died from Indian arrows and exposure. One man returned to the wreck site and survived. Fray Marcos, wounded but alive, was buried by his companions with his face exposed so that he might breathe until he succumbed. The Indians overlooked him and, reviving, Fray Marcos left his premature grave with maggots in his wounds to reach safety at the village of Tampico. He lived for thirty more years, with the stone chips of arrows embedded beneath his skin, and told his story.[1]

Spanish salvage of the wrecks began in two months and divers hooked onto box after box of silver bullion. It is estimated that they recovered about forty percent of the cargo. They retrieved what they could; the rest was abandoned and forgotten. Forgotten, that is, until 1967, when fortune hunters found the wreckage of the *Espíritu Santo*. Shell hunters had for years found

PADRE ISLAND NATIONAL SEASHORE

Padre Island National Seashore is one of the longest stretches of primitive, undeveloped ocean beach in the United States. It encompasses the greater part of the island located along the south Texas coast that runs north to south 100 miles from Corpus Christi to Port Isabel. Like other barrier islands, it is a dynamic place where one can witness change—change wrought by gentle breezes, by crashing waves, by tides, and, most dramatically, by the battering of violent storms and hurricanes.

The plants and animals are well adapted to these changes. Sea oats, for example, thrive here, setting their roots in the loose sand where few other plants can grow. With the sand anchored by the roots, other plants take hold, and in this way the dunes grow sometimes to thirty or forty feet in height and provide cover and nesting grounds for creatures of the island.

For those who enjoy swimming, sun bathing, fishing, camping, or discovering sea shells in the surf, this area is a veritable paradise. For those who enjoy his-

tory, Padre Island has many stories to tell of small native tribes who hunted and fished here, of shipwrecks, of hurricanes, of cattle ranches, and even of oil and gas exploration. The visitor may learn their stories at the visitors' center and on self-guided tours through well-marked trails. But how did the island get its name?

Alonso Alvarez de Pineda named it Isla Blanca in 1519 and, among several other names, it was also called Isla de Corpus Christi. In 1804, when Padre Jose Nicolas Balli founded a settlement on the island called Rancho Santa Cruz, the people began to call it Padre Balli's Island. Padre Balli built a mission at the ranch to christianize the native Karankawas and to serve the small community of ranch hands. After the padre's death, as a result of shifting sand and many hurricanes the ranch disappeared, its ruins to be discovered in 1931. Today the site is called the Lost City of Padre Island. In 1979, in recognition of Padre Balli's outstanding achievements and accomplishments, a historical marker honoring him was placed at the entrance to Padre Balli Park on Padre Island.

encrusted coins on the remote beach, and when engineers made a ship channel cut through Padre Island for Port Mansfield between 1957 and 1962 they dredged straight through the wreckage of the *Santa María de Yciar*. The only artifacts recovered were an anchor and a 2-real coin.[2] The site of the 1554 disaster, however, became obvious.

Platero, a treasure-hunting company from Gary, Indiana, began excavations on the *Espíritu Santo* in 1967. Court order, however, stopped the company's salvage operation in 1968 because it was working in tidelands owned by the state and because it was disturbing archeological remains. Platero turned over its treasure of silver coins, silver bullion, a gold bar, astrolabes, and ships' parts to the Texas Archeological Research Laboratory, and the state reimbursed the company $313,000. A 1969 State Antiquities Code established a special committee to control salvage and excavation on all state lands in the future, and between 1972 and 1975 state archeologists excavated the site of *San Esteban*.[3] Although it can be doubted if all the treasure—the Spanish had left some sixty percent of it—was recovered, the archeological discoveries were priceless. They rank among the earliest nautical artifacts of Spain in the New World. For Padre Island, however, the real treasure was to be found in recreation and tourism.

Ownership of the island, not counting Indian use, was granted by the Spanish monarch to Nicolás Ballí in 1759 and confirmed by the Mexican government in 1829 to Ballí's grandson, Padre José Nicolás Ballí and his nephew Juan José Ballí. Hence the name "Padre Island." The enterprising cleric early in the century established a church for Karankawa Indians and a ranch on the southern part of the island. Padre Island remained a part of Mexico until the Treaty of Guadalupe Hidalgo in 1848, and then the State of Texas recognized the rights of the Ballí family. John Singer and his wife, Johanna, bought land from the Ballís during the 1850s, but the Civil War forced them out. The Singers left behind only a legend of treasure buried in jars, lost in the shifting sands. In the 1870s Patrick Dunn gradually acquired most of the island for ranching purposes, constructed a home from driftwood, caught rainwater in an old whiskey barrel, and

fought a continual battle with trespassers who wanted to fish, hunt, and swim there. He even placed ads in the Brownsville and Corpus Christi newspapers warning people away. The idea of recreational use persisted, however, and Dunn sold development rights to Samuel A. Robertson in 1926.[4]

Colonel Robertson was a railroad and real-estate developer in the Rio Grande Valley who had fought as a scout for General "Blackjack" Pershing in Mexico. He was captured by Pancho Villa, dragged behind a horse, beaten up, and left for dead. He recovered, however, served in World War I as a rail builder, and was promoted to the rank of colonel. Afterward, he was sheriff of Cameron County, but his dream was to develop Padre Island as a resort area as he had done with the Del Mar hotel on Brazos Island. In 1927 he constructed a wooden bridge with open troughs for automobile tires, fourteen inches wide and fourteen inches deep, and partly filled with sand, from the mainland to the north end of Padre Island. Tourists placed their tires in the troughs and drove across three miles of water. It was called the Don Patricio Causeway in honor of Patrick Dunn. He also built a bridge between Padre and Mustang islands, put up two hotels near the southern end of Padre Island, and planned a road down the center of the island. The Great Depression and a hurricane in 1933 destroyed the hotels, the causeway, and the dream. It left the island isolated again, and only the ranching of the Dunn family remained.

Robertson, meanwhile, sold out to Albert and Frank Jones of Kansas City.[5] Following World War II, Albert Jones, along with M. E. Allison, formed the Padre Island Development Company to sell lots on the north end of the island. The lots sold but remained bare of houses, and the company passed through several ownerships. County bonds, however, provided for the construction of a new causeway in 1950. This opened public access to the island and two million people visited north Padre in the next four years. Eventually, in 1969, some condominiums and a hotel were built on the Gulf side behind a 4,200-foot-long, 15-foot-high, stepped concrete seawall. Banks were wary about financing construction until National Flood Insurance in 1968 and home insurance from the Texas Windstorm Catastrophe Pool in 1971 became available.[6] This stimulated building in coastal locations, and an expensive subdivision located around marinas slowly emerged on the bay side. The northern portion of the island, however, did not grow in a sensational manner like the southern part.

There had been little tourist interest at the southern tip of Padre Island, although Point Isabel on the mainland had long been a small summer resort for the heat-wilted farmers of the Rio Grande Valley. A small community developed before the Civil War and the brick landmark lighthouse was put up in 1852. Union ships raided the port during the Civil War to discourage blockade running, but their main target was the trade on the Rio Grande. River steamers brought Confederate cotton downstream from Brownsville to the mouth, where the boats were stopped by sandbars. Lighters carried the bales across to Brazos Island, a peninsular extension reaching from the mouth of the river northward toward Padre Island and Point Isabel. Here they were loaded on blockade runners which used Brazos Santiago Pass, between Brazos Island and Padre Island, to slip unnoticed into the Gulf of Mexico. The U.S. raids in 1863 merely forced the trade into Mexico and the shipment of cotton onto ships of neutral registry. A hurricane in 1867 destroyed the facilities on Brazos Island.[7]

Following the war, Point Isabel remained a small resort town with several restaurants and a hotel. It became "Port Isabel" in 1928 during the dredging of a shallow-draft canal. The harbor waters were eventually deepened, but the creation of a seventeen-mile ship channel to make Brownsville an inland port between 1934 and 1936 overshadowed the ambition at Port Isabel. Its future was tourism and in 1954, financed by Cameron County, the first Queen Isabella Causeway opened to South Padre Island. This gave automobile access to the island and opportunity to John L. Tompkins.

Tompkins, a thin, cigarette-smoking real-estate businessman from Corpus Christi, recognized the potential of Padre Island after camping there. "There was an absolutely untouched strip of land with a climate just as good as Miami's and a great deal better than anything the West Coast could offer," he said.[8] Tompkins studied Florida developments and began to buy land on the island. He lobbied for the building of the causeway, and when it opened Tompkins put up the first house for himself and began to sell lots. The early houses were made of cinder block on slab foundations; a few of those remain.

Resort construction began in 1955 with restaurants and hotels. There were fifteen resort hotels by the time the first condominiums appeared in the mid-1960s. South Padre Island boomed with the insurance changes to cover flood and wind damages, and it incorporated as a city in 1973. In the early 1980s the first Spring Break students arrived. There were 95,000 in 1983. There are now close to 250,000, largely through the month of March.[9] It was good business, but it required skill to handle the large masses of drunken, rowdy, sun-burned young adults temporarily forgetting the responsibilities of term papers and final exams. There have been rapes and fatal falls from balconies. On one occasion a drunken student, thinking it was a taxi, climbed into the back of a police car. Even after explanation, the muddled young man demanded to be taken to a nightclub, so the policeman took him to jail.[10]

South Padre Island, along with the rest of the Texas Gulf Coast, is subject to damage by storms. With its high-rise apartments and low elevation it seems particularly vulnerable. At the most, the town is a little over ten feet above sea level and, consequently, hotels have built individual sea walls, often as the front part of their structure. Most are seven to eight feet high. In 1960, Tompkins himself built a five-foot wall to protect his home and his subdivision. He had already bulldozed the dunes in front. In 1961 Hurricane Carla topped the wall, washed away his front yard, and exposed the concrete pillars of his house. In 1967 Hurricane Beulah undermined the seawall and broke it into pieces. Originally, the barrier was two hundred feet from the high tide line; by 1980 it was in the surf line.[11] Hurricane Allen in 1980 completed the destruction of Tompkins's house and it was bulldozed in 1983. Allen, a major storm, grazed South Padre on its way to Brownsville, but flattened the dunes and inflicted $40 million in damages.[12] This episodic erosion of the beach at South Padre, among the worst along the Texas coast, finally required correction with beach nourishment by the Corps of Engineers in 1997.[13]

Although the real-estate development of Padre Island needed concrete armor and special insurance to support human habitation, it was easy to foresee the same sort of coastal building that strangled the Florida beaches—high-rise apartments built side by side to the edge of the beach. That was Tompkins's dream, and also Robertson's in an earlier period. The middle portion of Padre Island, however, escaped such a fate because of a counter notion to preserve the island in a natural state for the enjoyment of future generations. This was a modern conservation impulse which offset the historical exploitation of nature by American business. The result was the Padre Island National Seashore.

There are several strands in the story of this preservation effort. One of them results from a democratic instinct to protect the rights of the public. The 1959 state Open Beaches Act, inspired by a national concern for the shorelines, gave the public the right to use the beaches from the low-tide line to the vegetation line of the dunes. Thus, hotels or home owners in Galveston, Bolivar, or South Padre, for example, could not fence off part of a beach for their private use. Moreover, if the beach shifted position, as it often does with storms, the public retained its right of access wherever the beach might form. There was also a growing conservation concern about wildlife and endangered species. Hence the passage of game laws in the early part of the century and the creation of the Aransas refuge to protect the whooping cranes and other migrating birds. This interest in wildlife was publicized by such individuals as Connie Hagar of Rockport, who counted birds twice a day for thirty-five years, and Ila Loetscher, the turtle lady of South Padre.

Loetscher, an adventuresome lady from Iowa—the first woman of that state to earn a pilot's license to fly—moved to the island in 1955 and became interested in the plight of the Kemp's ridley sea turtle. Numbers of the benign creatures had dropped due to raids by predators—human and otherwise—on their beach nesting areas in northern Mexico. Loetscher began to help sick and injured ridleys stranded on the beach at South Padre. She built tanks in her back yard, gave "Meet the Turtles" shows to tourists, and publicized the needs of the animals through a nonprofit organization, Sea Turtle, Inc. Efforts to enhance the turtles' survival followed in 1978 with protection of the Mexican nesting sites and the transfer of 2,000 eggs per year for ten years to Padre Island to establish a new nesting area. It takes about a decade for a ridley to mature and return to its instinctual nesting site. It was hoped that the turtles would return to Padre. Also, in 1992, the federal government began requiring turtle-excluder devices (TEDs) on commercial fishing nets to allow sea turtles to escape. The TEDs were a bother to shrimpers, but turtle deaths declined. In 1996 rangers found five nests on Padre Island and nine in 1997, not conclusive proof of the success of the experiment, but a glimmer of hope.[14]

These events and others—such as Lady Bird Johnson's interest in wildflowers and beautification, annual volunteer beach cleanups which started in Texas in 1986, the endangered species list, and front-page articles about the damage of oil spills to wildlife—measure a further cultural shift in support of conservation and preservation. In this post-World War II climate, the politicians created the Padre Island National Seashore, but it was not a new idea. D. E. Colp, the chair of the State Parks Board, suggested a park between Corpus Christi and Port Isabel in 1936. W. E. Pope of Corpus Christi introduced a bill in the Texas legislature, but Governor James Allred vetoed the measure because he thought the state already owned the land. Subsequent court rulings upheld private ownership, and the matter was dropped.

In 1955, as the north and south ends of the island began to undergo real-estate development, the National Park Service published *The Vanishing Shoreline*, which pointed out the loss of coastline in the United States to private interests. In 1958, subsequently, liberal Democrat Senator Ralph W. Yarborough of Texas introduced a bill to establish a national park on Padre Island, and President John F. Kennedy supported it in a speech to Congress recommending public seashore recreation areas. In

POINT ISABEL

Port Isabel, as it is called today, was originally known as El Fronton de Santa Isabel. It was a tiny village situated on a low bluff overlooking Laguna Madre, not far from the mouth of the Rio Grande River. Before the war with Mexico the name had changed to Point Isabel. Although the U.S. troops who camped there at the site of the lighthouse in 1848 referred to it as Fort Polk, that name was forgotten when the troops left at the end of the war.

Ships carrying the army's men and supplies from New Orleans anchored in the Gulf, and small steam and sail boats, called lighters, transported the goods and people across the shallows of Laguna Madre to Point Isabel.

Four brothers from Rovigno D'Istria, in northern Italy, served on the ships during that time. Their original name was Campeoni, and the men of the family had been seamen for generations. To avoid having her sons conscripted into the occupying Austrian army, their mother had sent five of her six boys to America. Two of them, Peter and Albert, met and married two Solis sisters, Felicitas and Estefania, whose family owned a ranch near Port Isabel. A third brother, Nicho-

las, joined them and they all entered into the life of the community, becoming merchants, hotel owners, and boat builders. The fourth brother, Andrew, caught gold fever and, despite the family's pleas, headed for California in 1849.

The youngest brother, Joseph, had a son, Charles Champion, who opened a mercantile company in 1894 and who, in 1899, built the imposing New Orleans–style structure shown in the painting to house his trade and his family. In the early part of this century he employed artist Jose Morales to paint pictures of sea life on the front walls of his building. The paintings are still there today. The mercantile store was not only the meeting place for the community, it was the place to buy fine imports, food, building materials, and other goods from all over the world. Charles Champion even had a railroad built that terminated in front of his business and it is said he minted his own money.

Today, this building has been lovingly restored and houses the Port Isabel Historical Museum, providing a glimpse of the history of the area as well as of the Champion family.

the hearings, Hector P. Garcia, a Corpus Christi physician and spokesman for the rights of the poor, commented: "For many hundreds of thousands of poor citizens in this area Padre Island is the only recreational area available to them . . . to some of these Mexican children the only gems and jewels in their life will be the beautiful shells they will find in this, our natural land."[15]

Ralph Yarborough testified in the same hearings:

We in Texas do not want a Miami type of development here with stone fences run out from hotels and motels across the beaches and down into the ocean fencing away from the beaches and the water all the people except those in a few high-priced private motels. The right to go down to the sea is a natural right and should be recognized as one of the inalienable rights of man. Buying and selling, buying and selling the beaches, buying and selling the ocean, what does it mean to us in the United States? If people are fenced away, of what value is that; is that right?[16]

Texas conservative Republican Senator John Tower, state's rights advocates, and land developers opposed the bill or tried to diminish it. John Tompkins of South Padre wanted a smaller park and argued, "With it we must have private development, motels, hotels, homes, towns, and cities."[17] Padre Island National Seashore, nonetheless, became law in 1962. Years of condemnation proceedings and civil suits followed, with a settlement of $23 million for the surface rights of 67.5 miles in the center of Padre Island. At the dedication in 1968, Lady Bird Johnson commented, "It has been said that wilderness is the miracle that man can tear apart, but cannot reassemble. So, I hope very much that these white sands, this dazzling dome of sky will be here, in all their freshness to be savored year after year."[18]

The National Park Service placed a visitor's center at the north end of Padre Island near Corpus Christi. The nearby beach provided recreation for day-trippers, and the rangers offered a wealth of information about the island, camping, and wildlife. The park was kept in its wild state with only a semi-annual cleanup to rid the beach of the trash that floated in with the tides. This flotsam and jetsam, which accumulates at a rate of two-and-a-half tons per mile per year, included drums of toxic chemicals, bales of marijuana, hypodermic needles, and plastics of great variety.[19] It was a reminder that humans have long used the sea as a dumping ground and that "civilization" was not far away.

In the middle of Padre Island, at the national seashore, nonetheless, preserved solitude can be found in the hand of nature. The restless wind blows the dry sand to reshape the beige dunes and the pounding surf measures the rhythmical heartbeat of the Gulf. The human visitor is more of an observer—accepted, perhaps, but not needed for nature to do its work. The rules are different there and human survival would be hard. In contrast, on the ends of the island are the amenities of urban life—air conditioning, automobiles, streets, drinkable water, music, television, hamburgers—a world shaped to human dimension where nature is kept at a distance. Both of the worlds of Padre Island are necessary for Texans and humanity—one to show where we have come from, the other to reveal what we have come to, in the progress of time.

AFTERWORD

Following the Fourth of July weekend in 1997, which brought some 100,000 people to South Padre Island and jammed the causeway for three hours, I returned for another visit to Boca Chica beach at the mouth of the Rio Grande. Not much had changed in six years. For twenty miles from Brownsville, Highway 4 still led across barren tidal flats and small rises covered with yucca, mesquite, and small live oak trees. Vegetation tends to hug the ground in this heated, searing climate as if pushed down by the hot hand of nature.

Twelve miles from the beach was a historical marker indicating that in May 1865, more than a month after the surrender of Robert E. Lee, the last battle of the Civil War was fought at this place. Union forces held Brazos Island (Boca Chica) and unrepentant Confederate soldiers occupied Brownsville. Texas commanders refused to recognize Lee's surrender as the termination of the war and when northern troops marched toward Fort Brown to take it over, southern soldiers, those who had not given up and gone home, met them halfway at Palmito Ranch. Rebel cavalry charges and artillery bombardment forced the exposed Yankee infantry on the flat land to retreat to their Brazos Island base. With that, Colonel "Rip" Ford told his Texas soldiers, "Boys, we have done finely. We will let well enough alone and retire."[1] A few days later officers arranged a truce, and soon Texas gave up. The Confederacy had won the last battle, but lost the war. The Battle of Palmito Ranch was a useless gesture, particularly for the fifty-five or so men injured or killed in the four-hour fight.

Symbolically, this countryside behind the beach was without much sign of human utilization. Traffic was slight, there were no fences and few houses, and there were no amenities of settled life except the narrow, asphalt highway itself. As it cut through the thirty-foot-high dunes, the same warning signs as appeared before appeared again to caution drivers about the abrupt end of the pavement. Only one family, five kids and four adults, Mexican-American, with a tent and camper, and a long line of trash barrels maintained by Cameron County occupied the broad beach. There was no feral dog to greet me as there had been on the first visit in 1991, but there were dog tracks in the loose sand around the holes of ghost crabs. Plastic forks and knives, cigarette butts, a rubber sandal, a beer bottle, and bits of charcoal were scattered among the few shells of the surf line. Light plastic bags, caught in the sea oats and primrose vines of the dunes, bellowed in the wind. Contrasting to the white-blue of the mid-morning sky, the sea was blue-green and the straight line of the horizon ended abruptly in the north with the distant, hazy, block-like high-rise apartments of South Padre Island.

Anyone who has looked at and studied the Gulf Coast must come to certain conclusions about the human use of the coastline. The weather can be hostile, destructive, and unforgiving. Hurricanes have been decisive in the history of Port Arthur, Bolivar, Galveston, Matagorda Bay, and Corpus Christi. Galveston and Corpus Christi have constructed seawalls for protection and there have been disjointed attempts at walled concrete armor on North and South Padre Island. In the twentieth century, the construction at Galveston, North Padre Island, and Corpus Christi has proven successful, albeit with the loss of beach sand. Yet none of these places has been struck by a category-five storm.

Since 1975 the National Weather Service has ranked hurricanes according to the Saffer/Simpson scale, which measures their destructive potential. This involves a judgment about sustained air speeds and the height of the storm tide created by the wind and the lowering of barometric pressure. Category one is the most moderate, with wind speeds of 74–95 m.p.h. and a tide of 4–5 feet. Category two is 96–110 m.p.h., with a 6–8-foot surge; category three is 111–130 m.p.h. and a 9–12-foot rise; category four is considered extreme, with winds of 131–155 m.p.h. and a tide of 13–18 feet; category five is rare and catastrophic, with winds over 155 m.p.h. and a tide over 18 feet. The purpose of the designations is to forewarn residents and emergency workers, but the classifications also provide a basis for historical analysis.

The problem is that the measurements are often imprecise due to the varying location of instruments, destruction of equip-

FRUITS OF THE SEA

The pot is boiling, the crabs and shrimp are turning red and pink, the onions, okra, and tomatoes are being prepared. Gumbo's on the menu. Of course, this is only one way to enjoy these and other marvelous fruits of the sea. Chefs have spent a lifetime creating such culinary masterpieces with crabs and shrimp as crab louie, etoufee, bisque, and much, much more.

Although there are many varieties of shrimp found in the Gulf, the most common are the brown and the white. As well as serving shrimp at the table, many fishermen prefer live shrimp as bait to catch trout and red snapper.

Blue crabs are found from Nova Scotia to northern Argentina, but are most common in the tidal marsh estuaries of the Gulf coast, where they prefer a moderate salinity. Although they are caught commercially, it is more fun to scoop up a net full of these beauties for the day's catch.

I have fond childhood memories of setting out crab nets on a warm summer afternoon and pulling up a net full of beautiful blue claw crabs. But watch out! Pick them up from the back or those beautiful blue claws will make a meal of your finger.

ment, and shifts in the storm. For example, the anemometer at Galveston in 1900 blew over at 84 m.p.h. (category one), had a storm surge of 14.5 feet (category four), and registered a barometer reading of 28.48 (category three). Current weather experts retrospectively rank the Galveston hurricane as category four.[2] Hurricane Allen, that skirted the Texas coast in August 1980, was category five (more than 155 m.p.h.) and weakened just before striking land thirty miles north of Brownsville in lightly populated country. It is considered the most intense and dangerous hurricane ever measured for Texas—it had a double eye in the center and a near-record low barometer reading of 26.55. Normal readings at sea level are 29.90; the 1935 killer hurricane of the Florida Keys set the record low at 26.35. Just passing by, Allen washed away the campsites at the national seashore, made sixty-eight cuts through South Padre, and inflicted about $296 million in total damage.[3] What would have happened if Allen had turned and come ashore with full force at South Padre Island? Would the high-rises been left leaning or toppled in the sand? What would have been the loss of life?

When Hurricane Camille, a category-five storm, struck the Louisiana-Mississippi coast in 1969, it had winds of 190–200 m.p.h. and tides of 22–25 feet. It killed 256 people and caused $1.42 billion in property damage. Hurricane frequency, however, varies along the Texas coast from one every twelve to fourteen years on the southern portion to one every seven to eight years on the northern part. Category-five hurricanes are rare—there have only been two in the twentieth century.[4] So, given the odds, a catastrophic hurricane would probably not strike South Padre Island, or Corpus Christi, or Galveston. Probably not—but it could. There are no guarantees in the mathematics of probability. A category-five storm can come during any hurricane season and could easily top the seawalls at Corpus Christi and Galveston. Then what? It is possible, and periodic destruction by hurricanes is a historical fact that should not be forgotten.

There are Cassandras who decry any construction or permanent living on the beach. One such is Roberto Garza, a geogra-

pher who studied the historic land use of Padre Island. He recommended in the conclusion of his 1980 dissertation the following: no sea walls; no insurance; no government financing of roads, water, or sewerage; no driving on the sand.[5] The most notorious critic, however, is Orrin H. Pilkey, Jr., a marine geologist from Duke University. The stout, combative professor has spoken and written repeatedly about the foolishness of interfering with the natural dynamics of shorelines. "It serves no critical societal purpose for people to live on the beach. In fact, it's really stupid to live so close to the beach when you can live back there a bit, live in a much safer situation, and then come over here and enjoy it. But Americans have it pounded into their heads that living in a beachfront cottage is the ultimate end point of modern life."[6] Pilkey has denigrated seawalls, beach replenishment, and shoreline housing. As might be expected, Pilkey is passionately hated by coastal real-estate developers, beach communities, and the U.S. Corps of Engineers.

The Cassandras are correct, of course. It is stupid to live on the beach. The sand-barrier islands are moving, rolling over themselves in storms, accumulating sand in one spot, losing it in another. There is no permanency; nature does not recognize the rights of private property. In the history of the Texas Coast those people who thought they could build lasting structures on the beach for pleasure or profit repeatedly have been proven wrong. Such people, nonetheless, in the last third of the twentieth century have been supported by federal flood insurance, and in Texas by an insurance pool forced to issue policies for wind damage. Taxpayers and other insurance owners, federal and state, therefore, have made possible the real-estate development on Padre Island, Galveston, Bolivar, and elsewhere. Citizens living nowhere near the coast have allowed "Mr. Henry Gotgold" to sit on his third-story balcony overlooking the Gulf and watch dolphins perform for his private pleasure. His house, located several feet above water, is insured and obviously vulnerable. How smart is that? Why did the politicians pass such laws? Cities and counties have poured money into causeways, bridges, and beach replenishment. Is that wise? The U.S. Corps of Engineers has used its engineering talent to shore up the coastline as well as make it profitable for industry. Was that all necessary?

It may be that a resort community like Galveston or South Padre should invest in beach nourishment, even with the knowledge that the sand will have to be replenished over and over again as the waves wash it away. It is an investment that will probably pay for itself if the storms stay away for a while. There is always a risk. Tourists, however, like a day at the beach. It is the major attraction of the Texas coast for travelers, and the tourist industry is the state's second largest employer. Thus, while it may be hard to rationalize insurance support for private homes built along the shore, a stronger argument, economic to be sure, can be made for the general investment of tax monies for tourist and port enhancement. This seems much more egalitarian, democratic, and beneficial for the general population.

Texans have reached a three-part balance in their use of the coastline. Port Arthur, Texas City, Brazosport, Port Lavaca, Corpus Christi, and the Intracoastal Canal are examples of economic designation where people can work and companies can profit. People also need to expand their dimensions of living. This involves recreation, and places such as Sea Rim, Bolivar,

Galveston, Rockport, and Padre Island are examples of that impulse. Beyond the use for jobs and leisure, Texans have expressed, in addition, a desire to preserve the future, to reach beyond the selfish present. The Aransas Pass Refuge with its whooping cranes and Padre Island National Seashore with its ridley turtles reveal that element of the balance. It remains to be seen how well this three-sided division of jobs, leisure, and conservation will serve the future, but it is nonetheless firmly in place.

There is a need for people to visit the coast and experience periodic communion with the sea—it is healthy for the human spirit. That opportunity has been assured for the people by the state. Meditation while strolling across the sand, searching for sand dollars in the surf line, watching children build castles, gazing at the amazing line of the straight horizon, listening to the raucous noise of the laughing gulls, feeling the humid embrace of the sea breeze, floating in the pulse of the waves, watching other people, recognizing the power of nature, absorbing the warmth of the sun—these are the offerings of the beach that redeem the human spirit. These are the gifts that belong to all Texans, to all people.

SUGGESTED READING

Alperin, Lynn M. *Custodians of the Coast*. Galveston, Tex.: Galveston District, U.S. Army Corps of Engineers, 1977.

Baker, T. Lindsay. *The Lighthouses of Texas*. College Station: Texas A&M University Press, 1991.

Bedichek, Roy. *Karánkaway Country*. 2d ed. Austin: University of Texas Press, 1974.

Bomar, George W. *Texas Weather*. 2d ed. rev. Austin: University of Texas Press, 1995.

Chipman, Donald E. *Spanish Texas, 1591–1821*. Austin: University of Texas Press, 1992.

Cipra, David L. *Lighthouses and Light Ships of the Northern Gulf of Mexico*. Washington, D.C.: Department of Transportation, U.S. Coast Guard, 1976.

Daniels, A. Pat. *Bolivar! Gulf Coast Peninsula*. Crystal Beach, Texas: Peninsula Press, 1985.

Doughty, Robin W. *Return of the Whooping Crane*. Austin: University of Texas Press, 1989.

Dreyfus, A. Stanley. *Henry Cohen, Messenger of the Lord*. New York: Bloch Publishers, 1963.

Holland, F. Ross. *Great American Lighthouses*. Washington, D.C.: Preservation Press, 1989.

———. *America's Lighthouses; Their Illustrated History since 1716*. Brattleboro, Vt: S. Greene Press, 1972.

Malsch, Brownson. *Indianola*. Austin, Tex.: Shoal Creek Press, 1977.

McAlister, Wayne, and Martha K. McAlister. *Aransas: A Naturalist's Guide*. Austin: University of Texas Press, 1995.

———. *Matagorda Island: A Naturalist's Guide*. Austin: University of Texas Press, 1993.

McCampbell, Coleman. *Texas Seaport: The Story of the Growth of Corpus Christi and the Coastal Bend Country*. New York: Exposition Press, 1952.

McComb, David G. *Galveston, a History*. Austin: University of Texas Press, 1986.

———. *Texas, a Modern History*. Austin: University of Texas Press, 1989.

Miller, Ray. *Ray Miller's Galveston*. Houston: Cordovan Press, 1983.

Moffett, A. W., revised by Richard L. Benefield. *The Shrimp Fishery in Texas*. Austin: Texas Parks and Wildlife Department, Coastal Fisheries Branch, January 1990.

Morton, Robert A., Orrin H. Pilkey, Jr., Orrin H. Pilkey, Sr., and William J. Neal. *Living with the Texas Shore*. Durham, N.C.: Duke University Press, 1983.

Newcomb, W. W., Jr. *The Indians of Texas*. Austin: University of Texas Press, 1961.

Payne, Richard, and Geoffrey Leavenworth. *Historic Galveston*. Houston: Herring Press, 1985.

Ricklis, Robert A. *The Karankawa Indians of Texas: An Ecological Study of Cultural Tradition and Change*. Austin: University of Texas Press, 1996.

St. John, Bob. *South Padre: The Island and Its People*. Dallas: Taylor Press, 1991.

Tveten, John L. *The Birds of Texas*. Fredricksburg, Tex.: Shearer Publishing, 1993.

Walraven, Bill. *Corpus Christi: The History of a Texas Seaport*. Woodland Hills, Calif.: Windsor Press, 1982.

———. *El Rincon: A History of Corpus Christi Beach*. Corpus Christi: Texas State Aquarium, 1990.

Weise, Bonnie R., and William A. White. *Padre Island National Seashore*. Austin: University of Texas, Bureau of Economic Geology, 1980.

Wiggins, Melanie. *They Made Their Own Law*. Houston: Rice University Press, 1990.

Wilcox, R. Turner. *Five Centuries of American Costumes*. New York: Charles Scribner's Sons, 1963.

NOTES

INTRODUCTION

1. Federal Writers' Project, *The WPA Guide to Texas* (New York: Hastings, 1940; Austin: Texas Monthly, 1986), 515.
2. W. W. Newcomb, Jr., *The Indians of Texas* (Austin: University of Texas Press, 1961), 315–317, 321, 325.
3. Newcomb, *Indians of Texas,* 64–66, 67. Robert A. Ricklis, *The Karankawa Indians of Texas* (Austin: University of Texas Press, 1996), 6–8, 14–24.
4. Noah Smithwick, *The Evolution of a State* (Austin: University of Texas Press, 1983), 3.
5. Ricklis, *Karankawa Indians,* 101–109.
6. Darwin Spearing, *Roadside Geology of Texas* (Missoula, Mont.: Mountain Press, 1991), 41–44, 103.
7. A. Pat Daniels, *Bolivar! Gulf Coast Peninsula* (Crystal Beach, Tex.: Peninsula Press, 1985), 1, 75.
8. Kate Cambridge, *InBetween,* August 1982.
9. George W. Bomar, *Texas Weather* (Austin: University of Texas Press, 1983), 93.
10. Robert A. Morton et al., *Living with the Texas Shore* (Durham, N.C.: Duke University Press, 1983), 12–15.
11. Roy Bedichek, *Karánkaway Country,* 2d ed. (Austin: University of Texas Press, 1974), 2–3.

THE SABINE CROSSING

1. Ron Tyler, ed., *The New Handbook of Texas* (Austin: Texas State Historical Association, 1996), vol. 1, 476–477. Henri Folmer, "De Bellisle on the Texas Coast," *Southwestern Historical Quarterly,* 44 (October 1940): 205–223.
2. Andrew Forest Muir, "Dick Dowling and the Battle of Sabine Pass," *Civil War History,* 4 (December 1958): 419.
3. A. Pat Daniels, *Bolivar! Gulf Coast Peninsula* (Crystal Beach, Tex.: Peninsula Press, 1985), 33.
4. Keith L. Bryant, Jr., *Arthur E. Stilwell: Promoter with a Hunch* (Nashville: Vanderbilt, 1971), viii, 95–96, 158–161. Works

Projects Administration, American Guide Series, *Port Arthur* (Houston: Anson Jones, 1940), 29–35.
5. *Fort Worth Star-Telegram,* June 12, 1983. See also *Dallas Times-Herald,* November 12, 1978 (oil smell and white flight); *Dallas Morning News,* July 19, 1982 (downtown); *Houston Chronicle,* June 9, 1989 (air pollution); *Business Week,* April 23, 1990 (lung cancer); *Port Arthur News,* March 15, 1992 (ozone); *Community Post,* October 28, 1992 (lead).

THE BOLIVAR PENINSULA

1. Forest W. McNeir, *Forest McNeir of Texas* (San Antonio: Naylor, 1956), 32–35, 39, 44–46, 66, 68, 87.
2. Ron Tyler, ed., *The New Handbook of Texas* (Austin: Texas State Historical Association, 1996), 1: 627; 4: 274. Melanie Wiggins, *They Made Their Own Law* (Houston: Rice University Press, 1990), 51.
3. Wiggins, *They Made Their Own Law,* 34, 48–50. A. Pat Daniels, *Bolivar! Gulf Coast Peninsula* (Crystal Beach, Tex.: Peninsula Press, 1985), 36. See also T. Lindsay Baker, *Lighthouses of Texas* (College Station: Texas A&M University Press, 1991), 57–65.
4. Wiggins, *They Made Their Own Law,* 215.
5. Daniels, *Bolivar!,* 46–48; *New Handbook of Texas,* vol. 2: 1121.
6. Wiggins, *They Made Their Own Law,* 51–59.
7. Ibid., 56–65. Daniels, *Bolivar!,* 38.
8. Wiggins, *They Made Their Own Law,* 84–91; Baker, *Lighthouses,* 62–63.
9. Wiggins, *They Made Their Own Law,* 84–92.
10. Ibid., 92.
11. Daniels, *Bolivar!,* 40–45, 53–58.
12. Rogayle Franklin, "Autumn Flights of Fancy on Bolivar Peninsula," *Houston Chronicle,* November 26, 1995: 6–7.
13. *New Handbook of Texas,* 2: 430.

14. *Houston Chronicle*, June 28, 1959. *Austin American-Statesman*, August 15, 1987. Wiggins, *They Made Their Own Law*, 107.
15. *Houston Chronicle*, March 2, 1997.

GALVESTON ISLAND

1. Francis C. Sheridan, *Galveston Island, or a Few Months Off the Coast of Texas: The Journal of Francis C. Sheridan, 1839–1840,* ed. Willis W. Pratt (Austin: University of Texas Press, 1954), 53. Much of the information for this essay is taken from David G. McComb, *Galveston, a History* (Austin: University of Texas Press, 1986), and from David G. McComb, "Galveston as a Tourist City," *Southwestern Historical Quarterly,* vol. 100 (January 1997): 331–360.
2. Robert A. Morton, et al., *Living with the Texas Shore* (Durham, N.C.: Duke University Press, 1983), 24.

THE BRAZOS LANDING

1. Mary Austin Holley, *Texas* (Austin: Texas State Historical Association, 1990), 121–122.
2. T. R. Fehrenbach, *Lone Star* (New York: Macmillan, 1968), 172–173.
3. Pamela Ashworth Puryear and Nath Winfield, Jr., *Sandbars and Sternwheelers: Steam Navigation on the Brazos* (College Station: Texas A&M University Press, 1976), 17.
4. Holley, *Texas,* 32.
5. Puryear and Winfield, *Sandbars and Sternwheelers,* 20–23.
6. Marilyn McAdams Sibley, *Travelers in Texas, 1761–1860* (Austin: University of Texas Press, 1967), 33.
7. David G. McComb, *Texas, a Modern History* (Austin, University of Texas Press, 1989), 69.
8. See Kenneth E. Hendrickson, Jr., *The Waters of the Brazos: A History of the Brazos River Authority, 1929–1979* (Waco: Texian, 1981).

9. Susan Chester, ed., *The Lake Jackson Chronicles: A History of Lake Jackson, Texas* (Old Ocean, Tex.: Lake Jackson 50th Historical Committee, 1993), 6, 9, 11, 15, 22 (ditty), 86. Linda Wing, "The Town of Lake Jackson," typescript, October 28, 1993, 9, 10, 15.
10. For an example of the migrants, see William B. Seward, *East From Brazosport* (Midland, Mich.: Dow Chemical, 1974).

TROUBLED WATERS AT MATAGORDA BAY

1. Gary Cartwright, "Eerie Canal," *Texas Monthly,* vol. 24 (July 1996), 82–85. *Austin American,* June 18, 1949. Lynn M. Alperin, *Custodians of the Coast* (Galveston: Galveston District, U.S. Army Corps of Engineers, 1977), 151–172.
2. Matagorda County Historical Commission, *Historic Matagorda County* (Houston: D. Armstrong, 1986), vol. 1, 398.
3. *Gulf Intracoastal Waterway, Sargent Beach, Texas,* House Document 103-34 (Washington: U.S. Government Printing Office, 1993), 33–34, 58–64.
4. Cartwright, "Eerie Canal," 87.
5. Robert S. Weddle, *The French Thorn* (College Station: Texas A&M University Press, 1991), 26–39.
6. David Roberts, "In Texas, a Ship Is Found and a Grand Dream Recalled," *Smithsonian,* vol. 28 (April 1997): 41–52.
7. Mary A. Maverick, *Memoirs of Mary A. Maverick,* edited by Rena Maverick Green (Lincoln: University of Nebraska Press, 1989), 81.
8. Brownson Malsch, *Indianola* (Austin, Tex.: Shoal Creek, 1977), 6–7, 8–9, 228–237.
9. Malsch, *Indianola,* 248.
10. Matagorda County Historical Commission, *Historic Matagorda County,* vol. 1, 59, 274, 380, 398. *Austin American,* September 14, 1961 (quote).

THE ARANSAS PASSAGE

1. Wayne H. McAlister and Martha K. McAlister, *Aransas: a Naturalist's Guide* (Austin: University of Texas Press, 1995), 41–47.
2. Robin W. Doughty, *Return of the Whooping Crane* (Austin: University of Texas Press, 1989), 14.
3. John Russell Bartlett, *Personal Narrative of Explorations and Incidents in Texas, New Mexico, California, Sonora, and Chihuahua* (New York: D. Appleton, 1854), vol. 2, 533.
4. Robin W. Doughty, *Wildlife and Man in Texas* (College Station: Texas A&M University Press, 1983), 166–179.
5. Wayne H. McAlister and Martha K. McAlister, *Matagorda Island: a Naturalist's Guide* (Austin: University of Texas Press, 1993), 64–65, 73–82.
6. McAlister, *Aransas*, 76–87.
7. Frederick Law Olmsted, *A Journey Through Texas* (Austin: University of Texas Press, 1978), 135.
8. Robert Porter Allen, *On the Trail of Vanishing Birds* (New York: McGraw-Hill, 1957), 35.
9. Doughty, *Return of the Whooping Crane*, 26.
10. Allen, *On the Trail of Vanishing Birds*, 35–36.
11. Ibid., 212–213, 231.
12. Faith McNulty, *The Whooping Crane* (New York: Dutton, 1966), 27, 29, 45, 48, 49.
13. Jane Grandolfo, "Homing Instinct," *Texas Monthly*, vol. 22 (January 1994), 40–43. Quote from *Victoria Advocate*, September 19, 1991.
14. Richard C. Bartlett, *Saving the Best of Texas* (Austin: University of Texas Press, 1995), 108.
15. McNulty, *Whooping Crane*, 36–37.

CORPUS CHRISTI AND THE COWTOWNS OF THE COAST

1. Writer's Program, Works Projects Administration, *Corpus Christi: A History and Guide* (Corpus Christi: Caller-Times, 1942), 75. See also Robert H. Thonhoff, "Taylor's Trail in Texas," *Southwestern Historical Quarterly*, vol. 70 (July 1966), 7–22.
2. Bill Walraven, *Corpus Christi: The History of a Texas Seaport* (Woodland Hills, Calif.: Windsor, 1982), 39.
3. Walraven, *Corpus Christi*, 39. W. R. Gore, "The Life of Henry Lawrence Kinney," M.A. thesis (Austin: University of Texas, 1948), 131–132.
4. *Victoria Advocate*, January 6, 1985; *San Antonio Express Magazine*, December 27, 1953; Dorothy Louise Nims, "A History of the Village of Rockport," M.A. thesis (San Marcos: Southwest Texas Teachers College, 1939), 26–48.
5. Dana Shelton, "Rockport: Where Birds and Birders Flock Together," *Texas Highways* (March 1980): 18–20. See also Karen H. McCracken, *Connie Hagar* (College Station: Texas A&M University Press, 1986).
6. Lessoff, "Texas City and Texas Myth," 324–325. Coleman McCampbell, *Texas Seaport: The Story of the Growth of Corpus Christi and the Coastal Bend Country* (New York: Exposition, 1952), 66–67, 72.
7. Dan E. Kilgore, "Corpus Christi: A Quarter Century of Development, 1900–1925," *Southwestern Historical Quarterly*, vol. 75 (April 1972), 437, 438 (quote), 439.
8. McCampbell, *Texas Seaport*, 84–85. Walraven, *Corpus Christi*, 79–81. Kilgore, "Corpus Christi," 440.
9. Lynn M. Alperin, *Custodians of the Coast* (Galveston: Galveston District, United States Corps of Engineers, 1977), 134–135.
10. Writer's Program, WPA, *Corpus Christi*, 216–217.
11. Bill Walraven, *El Rincon: A History of Corpus Christi Beach* (Corpus Christi: Texas State Aquarium, 1990), 35–37, 51.
12. Ibid., 59–63.
13. Walraven, *Corpus Christi*, 9.
14. *Corpus Christi Caller-Times*, June 15, 1988.

PADRE ISLAND—SHIPWRECKS AND TOURISTS

1. Barto Arnold III and Robert Weddle, *The Nautical Archeology of Padre Island* (New York: Academic Press, 1978), 22, 27, 28, 38–48.
2. Ibid., 188.
3. Ibid. Dorris L. Olds, *Texas' Legacy from the Gulf* (Austin: Texas Memorial Museum and Texas Antiquities Committee, 1976), 1–4, 14–15, 151.
4. Roberto Garza, "An Island in Geographic Transition: A Study of the Changing Land Use Patterns of Padre Island, Texas," Ph.D. dissertation (Boulder: University of Colorado, 1980), 53–62.
5. Ibid., 62–66.
6. Ibid., 72–76, 117.
7. James W. Daddysman, *The Matamoros Trade: Confederate Commerce, Diplomacy and Intrigue* (Newark: University of Delaware Press, 1984), 29–33, 86–94, 180–186.
8. Padre Island Boosters' Club press release, 1959. In Padre Island vertical file, Center for American History, University of Texas.
9. Bob St. John, *South Padre: The Island and Its People* (Dallas: Taylor, 1991), 15–25, 226–232.
10. Elizabeth Sweeten, "Humorous Events," *The Official Spring Break Guide,* March 1991, 56.
11. Garza, *"An Island in Geographic Transition,"* 163–165.
12. St. John, *South Padre,* 27.
13. *Houston Chronicle,* March 2, 1997.
14. St. John, *South Padre,* 213–219. *USA Today,* June 20, 1996, July 17, 1997.
15. Padre Island National Park. Hearings before the Subcommittee on Public Lands, Committee on Interior and Insular Affairs, United States Senate, 86th Congress, 1st session. Corpus Christi, Texas, December 14, 1959 (Washington: Government Printing Office, 1960), 80.
16. Ibid., 9.
17. Ibid., 82.
18. *Corpus Christi Caller,* April 9, 1968. *Dallas Morning News,* April 4, 1962.
19. *USA Today,* May 25, 1990.

AFTERWORD

1. John Salmon Ford, *Rip Ford's Texas,* edited by Stephen B. Oates (Austin: University of Texas Press, 1987), 391.
2. Paul J. Hebert and Glenn Taylor, "The Deadliest, Costliest, and Most Intense United States Hurricanes of this Century," *NOAA Technical Memorandum* (Miami: National Hurricane Center, 1978), 4. See also Robert H. Simpson and Herbert Riehl, *The Hurricane and Its Impact* (Baton Rouge: Louisiana State University Press, 1981), 218, 366–369.
3. U.S. Army Corps of Engineers, Galveston, Texas, "Report on Hurricane Allen, 3–10 August 1980" (Galveston, 1981), 6–7, 13, 62. *Corpus Christi Caller,* August 8, 1980.
4. Simpson and Riehl, *The Hurricane,* 19, 21, 374.
5. Roberto Garza, "An Island in Geographic Transition: A Study of the Changing Land Use Patterns of Padre Island, Texas," Ph.D. dissertation (Boulder: University of Colorado, 1980), 186.
6. Kim A. McDonald, "A Geology Professor's Fervent Battle With Coastal Developers and Residents," *Chronicle of Higher Education,* October 6, 1993: A8.

RESOURCES

The following publications, books, and articles provided additional information for this book: *The Shrimp Fishery in Texas,* by A. W. Moffett, revised by Richard L. Benefield (Texas Parks and Wildlife Department, Coastal Fisheries Branch, January 1990); *The Texas Shrimp Fishery—A Report to the Governor and the 74th Legislature* (Texas Parks and Wildlife Department, January 1995); *"Elissa's Historic Voyage,"* by Ann Galloway (*Texas Highway Magazine,* July 1996); *The Blimp Base,* by John W. Mecom (including photos and descriptions for proposed purchase); *Padre Island National Seashore,* by Bonnie R. Weise and William A. White (University of Texas, Bureau of Economic Geology, Austin, 1980); *Return of the Whooping Crane,* by Robin W. Doughty (University of Texas Press, Austin, 1989); *Henry Cohen, Messenger of the Lord,* by A. Stanley Dreyfus (Bloch Publishers, New York, 1963); *Costume Through the Ages,* by Erhard Klepper and James Laver (Simon and Schuster, New York, 1963); *Five Centuries of American Costume,* by R. Turner Wilcox (Charles Scribner's Sons, New York, 1963); *The Encyclopedia of World Costume,* by Doreen Yarwood (Charles Scribner's Sons, New York, 1978); *The History of Sailing Ships* (Arco Publishers, New York); *The History of Ships,* by Peter Kemp (Orbis Publishers, London); *"Sieur de LaSalle's Fateful Landfall,"* by David Roberts (*Smithsonian Journal* 28(1) April 1997: 40; *Great American Lighthouses,* by F. Ross Holland, Jr. (Preservation Press, Washington, D.C., 1989); *America's Lighthouses; Their Illustrated History since 1716,* by F. Ross Holland, Jr.

(S. Greene Press, Brattleboro, Vt, 1972; Dover Publications, New York, 1981); *Lighthouses and Light Ships of the Northern Gulf of Mexico,* by David L. Cipra (Department of Transportation, U.S. Coast Guard, 1976); "Lights Ashore," by Bob Parvin (*Texas Highways Magazine,* September 1978); *Ray Miller's Galveston,* by Ray Miller (Cordovan Press, Houston, 1983); *Galveston—A History,* by David G. McComb (University of Texas Press, Austin, 1986); *Historic Galveston,* by Richard Payne and Geoffrey Leavenworth (Herring Press, Houston, 1985); *The Karankawa Indians of Texas: An Ecological Study of Cultural Tradition and Change,* by Robert A. Ricklis (University of Texas Press, Austin, 1996); *The Indians of Texas, from Prehistoric to Modern Times [1969],* by W. W. Newcomb, Jr. (University of Texas Press, Austin, 1993); *Karánkaway Country,* 2d ed., by Roy Bedichek (University of Texas Press, Austin, 1974); *Spanish Texas 1519–1821,* by Donald E. Chipman (University of Texas Press, Austin, 1992); *The Blue Crab Fishery of the Gulf of Mexico,* by Charles G. Moss (Texas Agricultural Service, Texas A&M University System); *Texas Blue Crab Fishery Management Plan* (Texas Parks and Wildlife Department, Coastal Fisheries Branch); *The Birds of Texas,* by John L. Tveten (Shearer Publishing, Fredericksburg, Tex., 1993); *Padre Island National Seashore* (Historic resource study—National Park Service, U.S. Department of the Interior, August 1971); *Padre Island Official Map and Guide* (National Park Service, U.S. Department of the Interior).